the Santal

the

A TRIBE

$Santal$

IN SEARCH OF A GREAT TRADITION

By **Martin Orans**

University of California, Riverside

WAYNE STATE UNIVERSITY PRESS, DETROIT, 1965

Contents

List of Tables vi / Acknowledgments vii / Introduction ix

1 TRADITIONAL SANTAL SOLIDARITY
1. The Internal Aspect of Solidarity 3 / 2. External Solidarity 27

2 THE MIGRATION TO INDUSTRIAL EMPLOYMENT
3. The Rise of Education 47 / 4. The Decline of Ceremonies 57 / 5. The Extent of Hindu Absorption 87

3 THE NEW SOLIDARITY
6. The Political Rank Path 93 / 7. The "Great Tradition" 105

4 THE RANK CONCESSION SYNDROME
8. The Theory of the RCS 123 / 9. Implications of the RCS 137

References 147

Index 151

Tables

1. *Number of Aborigine Pupils*   50
2. *Choice of Marriage Form by Farmers by Per-Capita Income*   66
3. *Choice of Marriage Form by* Bustee *Workers*   68
4. *Farmers and Workers Per Capita Agricultural Incomes*   70
5. *Percentage of Santal Returned as Hindu*   88

Acknowledgments

Like many another first book by an academic this one is a somewhat more literate account of material and ideas from my dissertation presented to the anthropology department of the University of Chicago in 1962. Though there is no place to begin in acknowledging the contributions of mentors, I am especially grateful to Milton Singer who served as chairman of my thesis committee and to Fred Eggan—both of whom steered me past as many reefs as they could. Manning Nash and Surajit Sinha similarly contributed at various points as members of the committee. Along the route crucial help was also provided by Robert Redfield, Fred Gearing, Gundar Frank, Morris Morris and McKim Marriott.

The fourteen months of field work in India and additional time for research which made this work possible were supported by funds from the Foreign Area Training Program of the Ford Foundation. Investigation of the effects of industrial employment on traditional tribal culture were greatly facilitated by the Tata Iron and Steel Company, which was generous in offering me its facilities and good offices.

Acknowledgments

As for the field work itself, I must first of all acknowledge the aid of Marian Orans, who was at the time my wife and full partner in field work. Without her efforts my work would have been very much impoverished. My field assistants, Pius Kisku and Pradhan Murmu, provided assistance far beyond the call of duty. Jai Pal Singh is also to be thanked for having helped to establish my *bona fides* among the Santal. The hospitality of so many other Indian friends shall here have to be acknowledged collectively.

Finally I must offer thanks to the Santal as a people for the great generosity they extended to me wherever I went. I think that I have learned from the Santal far more important things than I have been able to express in this book; but these things I carry about as part of myself.

M. O.

Introduction

Less than a decade ago the anthropologists Redfield and Singer offered their colleagues in the social sciences a set of constructs to aid in understanding the part cities play in the development of culture. From that offering the most salient constructs, judging by usage, have been the concepts of the "great tradition" and the "little tradition." Great traditions were regarded as the stuff of civilization and as having the qualities of explicitness, systematization and reflectiveness. Little traditions were conceived of as the product of folk societies and as relatively lacking in these qualities. But such constructs as great and little traditions are mainly aids to thought, and one hardly expects to encounter them as objects of experience, particularly in the very form in which they have been postulated. Imagine then my surprise at encountering a self-conscious effort to create a great tradition, precisely as Redfield and Singer define it, among a tribal people well known for having long managed to preserve a considerable degree of distinctiveness from the dominant surrounding civilized society.

This work is in large measure an effort to understand the

development and characteristics of this emergent great tradition. In seeking such understanding, attention has been focused on the shifting historical pressures for and against acculturation and assimilation, and on the impact of a spreading market economy, industrialization and political democracy. Though this is not at all a monograph purporting to tell all about a particular people, the events described are largely the experience of a single tribe, the Santal, who live primarily on the Chotanagpur Plateau of Bihar, West Bengal, and northern Orissa in India. This is, then, in part "their story," understood often in terms peculiar to their experience. Nevertheless, the experiences of the Santal suggest certain widely prevalent processes which I call the "rank concession syndrome." These processes are speculatively held to pertain to all part-societies which have conceded rank to a dominant surrounding society. In particular the pressures for and against assimilation are regarded as crucial determinants and these in turn are seen to depend significantly upon shifting avenues of mobility. Movements of self-conscious cultural creativity are viewed in relation to the conflicting stimuli generated by pressures for and against assimilation. There are adequate if not compelling theoretical and practical reasons for making the Santal the object of such a study. The characteristically primitive worldview and social organization of traditional Santal culture provides a sufficiently contrasting background against which to view the impact of such modern conditions as the market, industrial employment and political democracy. Similarly the heavy commitment to pursuit of pleasure and the characteristically unreflective character of traditional Santal culture contrast sharply with the dominant surrounding Brahmanical tradition. Their patterns of social interaction and group structure rest heavily upon a markedly patrilineal kinship system closely paralleling that of their Hindu neighbors. On the other hand, their social organization is relatively lacking in the cleavages of caste which are so prevalent all about them. Apart from the village, which is usually composed of a number of patrilineal kin-groups, territorial organization is weakly developed, and the tribe as a whole has never been politically unified so far as historical records indicate.

Even as a unique people the Santal merit special attention. Numbering today over three million, the region they occupy contains the richest deposits of iron, coal and other crucial industrial minerals in all of India. The chief source of their livelihood, at least since the nineteenth century, has been settled agriculture. Prior to the nineteenth century, hunting was also an important livelihood activity, but the great increase in the region's population and subsequent reduction of forest areas has made game extremely scarce; it is now difficult for the inhabitants even to obtain materials for fuel and building purposes. Though the chief source of food and cash is the annual rice crop, a few vegetables are also grown and some fruit trees maintained. Some villages are near enough to a river for fish to be readily obtained, while some villages stock their local ponds. Even prior to the introduction of modern industry in the region, the Santal had ceased to be economically independent. Although they once did some pottery making, weaving, and even iron smelting, they have come to rely almost exclusively on various local Hindu castes for these material products. Women from several low Hindu castes are used frequently as midwives. While almost no Santal are ritually served by Brahmin priests, itinerant Hindu holy men (*sadhu*) visit many Santal villages, consulting horoscopes and offering prayers for a fee or donation.

Most Santal are still agriculturists, but some have turned to less time-honored work. The chief industry in which these others are employed is as characteristically modern as the Santal themselves are not. It is the Tata Iron and Steel Company (TISCO), the largest and oldest modern iron and steel company in India. Since Santal have been employed by TISCO from its founding over fifty years ago, enough time has elapsed for change to become manifest and for the directions of change to become evident.

Jamshedpur, the industrial town which was created to house TISCO, was carved out of the jungle of Singhbhum district, Bihar, in 1908; it owes its location to the rich natural resources of the surrounding area, in which the Santal and other closely related tribes form a substantial part of the population. The population of the city has been drawn from every section of India as well as a number of foreign countries and has grown to more than 218,000. Jamshedpur is extremely atypical compared to other Indian cities—the fact that it is a company town of unprecedented size accounts in large measure for its atypicality. TISCO has from the beginning completely controlled the government of the town, provided housing for most of its workers, operated a school system, and furnished other services. It is a city as much dominated by modern industry as a medieval city was by its cathedral. Traditional institutions, such as temples and socio-political organizations, exist but are weakly developed; the Tata Company, the Tata Workers Union, and the town's competing regional and national political parties are the dominant corporate groups. Caste persists as an institution for regulating marriage, for assigning employment in certain traditionally degrading occupations, and to a certain extent in structuring social interaction. But class in the traditional Western sense is increasingly displacing caste as the organizing principle of membership in social groups and in social interaction.

It is chiefly the southern Santal from the territories adjacent to Jamshedpur who have contributed to its working force, and these are the Santal with whom I have done field work. They come largely from the Dhalbhum subdivision of the Singhbhum district in Bihar, the Mayurbhanj district of Orissa, and from the former princely states of Seraikela and Kharswan, now also in Singhbhum; a few have come from the Manbhum district of Bihar, north of Jamshedpur, and from the Midnapur district of Bengal on the east.

Since Santal industrial workers live both outside and within Jamshedpur, exceptional opportunities were available to compare separately the effects of industrial employment and living in an urban environment. Most of the Santal workers live outside the city of Jamshedpur in village-like settlements (*bustees*) of their own construction. Some of these *bustees* were formerly traditional agricultural villages, while others have grown up only since the development of Jamshedpur and the influx of industrial workers. These settlements from which the workers commute daily to Jamshedpur lie from three to ten miles from the city. The smaller number of Santal workers who live within Jamshedpur either occupy Company houses scattered throughout the town or live in one of the *bustees* within the town. Though I spent considerable time with the city Santal occupying Company houses, I unfortunately did not have the time to make more than casual observations of the city *bustee* dwellers. Almost all Santal industrial workers, whether living in Jamshedpur or in a *bustee*, come from native villages within a fiftymile radius of Jamshedpur.

The *bustee* in which I did intensive field work, and which I shall call Daredih, was a traditional agricultural village long before Jamshedpur was built; it lies about three miles from the city and while it is the native village of some of its inhabitants, most are migrants from the surrounding countryside. Since even those for whom it is a native village (and who have adjoining agricultural land) generally work in Jamshedpur, it is possible to compare them with the migrant industrial workers so that the effects of migration may be examined. Exclusively rural villages lying far away from Jamshedpur constituted something of a base-line from which to view the urban-industrial effects of Jamshedpur on Santal culture. The rural village in which I spent the most time and which I shall call Fanderkuta, lies in Mayurbhanj about fifty miles from Jamshedpur. Other villages in Mayurbhanj and Seraikela were visited, and one in Mayurbhanj was repeatedly used for control purposes.

Since the subject matter at hand is cultural change, a broadly chronological order of presentation has been followed. The base line for change, though constructed from both historical accounts and contemporary observations of rural villages, is treated first. This is followed by an account of those changes associated with the market economy and migration to industrial employment. The most recent Santal historical experience, including the introduction of political democracy and the emergence of an indigenous great tradition, terminates the presentation of the facts of change. On the basis of this historical evidence and with an eye on general theoretical considerations, the final portion of this work is concerned with the rank concession syndrome and its various applications.

1
traditional santal solidarity

Chapter 1 The Internal Aspect of Solidarity

Solidarity is a Janus-faced deity: it has an internal and an external aspect. Internally it refers to the degree of social cooperation and mutual accommodation which a society manifests in performing its normal routine. Externally, solidarity refers to the ability of a society to stand as a unit against external encroachment. These two aspects of solidarity are, of course, intimately related; nevertheless it is a commonplace that societies badly lacking in internal solidarity may pull themselves together remarkably well in the face of a real, imagined, or even contrived external threat. Since this is so, and because one estimates the extent of internal and external solidarity by different observations, it is useful to make the distinction between the two in discussing Santal solidarity.

The internal solidarity of traditional Santal society has always depended importantly on what Durkheim has referred to as the principle of "likeness,"[1] i.e., those shared cultural characteristics which serve to bind together a society. In this context one thinks first of all of those shared symbols and symbolic

---

[1] Durkheim 1933:136

acts which represent and give recognition to existing social units. But apart from these official boundary markers, and perhaps even more important, are the "shared understandings" and the countless similar behavior patterns and similar material manifestations of behavior which characterize a people.

Among the cultural bonds which pertain to all Santal directly (as opposed to those which are exclusively the property of the various component social units of Santal society) is a myth of creation which comes as close to being an official symbol of unity and a constitution as traditional Santal society has attained. However there are numerous versions of this myth due to the wide dispersion of the Santal, and there are very few Santal who are in possession of more than fragments of a complete version. Culshaw reports that the myth is better known among the older generation and suggests that it is dying out; several ceremonies in which it is normally recited appear to be disappearing in the Bankura District of Bengal where Culshaw gathered his data.[2] Since there are also lengthy accounts of the myth in earlier works,[3] one is tempted to accept the conclusion that knowledge of the myth has declined generally. It must, however, be taken into account that it was formerly the custom to find informants who could elaborate an "authoritative" version of tradition. Also, it is often the case among the Santal, as others, that older men become specialists in ritual knowledge, so that absence of such knowledge among the young may not indicate that the knowledge is disappearing.

Since numerous accounts and several versions of the myth appear in the literature, only those major themes which are almost always present wherever there are Santal will be re-

[2] Culshaw 1949.
[3] Dalton 1872; Bodding 1942, originally 1887.

ported here. The origin of the Santal is attributed to a goose (*hãs*; Hindi, *hamsa* = gander) and a gander (*hãsil*; Hindi, *hamsa* = gander) which were made out of grass seeds (*sirom*) or lived in such grass. With the assistance of the deity known by the Bengali terms *Thakur* or *Mahaprobu* or *Thakur-Mahaprobu*, or by the Santali *Maran Buru* (literally "Great Mountain") the two eggs of the pair became the first "humans," i.e., Santal or *hor*. Like many other tribal peoples, the Santal refer to themselves as "people" (*hor*). Since there were no others, these two, in spite of being siblings, had to mate. It is said that Thakur had to teach them how to make rice beer (*Handi*) at this time so that they would get drunk since they were ashamed to have intercourse when sober, especially since they were siblings. There is often a lengthy account of the places to which this pair traveled, and the offspring they had at various places are named. Hihiri and Pipiri are always included prominently in these travels. The two ancestors are named Pilcu Haram and Pilcu Budhi (Hindi, *Hār* = bone) (Hindi, *Budhi* = old and/or wise), and they are said to have divided their offspring into twelve clans on the basis of various adventures. Sometimes these adventures are connected with the clan name and totemic food abstinence. The one occasion on which I heard a full account of the myth, unsolicited, was at a wedding, and it is clear from my inquiries that few present knew as much of the myth as was then recited.

The essential features of this myth are shared with the Ho and Munda, two closely related tribes speaking related Mundari languages and inhabiting territories adjacent to the Santal, or living intermingled with them. Other points of overlap between the Santal and these neighboring tribes will be indicated in this chapter.

5

If the future viability of the myth is open to question, that of the language bond is not. A common language is a bond whose strength can hardly be overestimated; for pervasiveness and necessity no bond can match it. There are dialectical differences, particularly between north and south; a few quite regular sound shifts may cause brief difficulties in communication, and a few words have different meanings or are known only in a particular region. Nevertheless, there is almost complete mutual intelligibility. The Santal themselves are deeply cognizant of language as a basis for intimacy and often indicated to me their desire that I properly learn their language. What little progress I made in this direction was greatly appreciated and always increased the intimacy which the Santal were willing to afford me. The much greater proficiency in Santali that my wife developed allowed her to be more of a Santal than I. As with the origin myth, Santali provides links with the neighboring Mundari-speaking people, though here intelligibility is not always satisfactory.

This is not the place to chronicle the numerous ceremonies, rituals, ritual paraphernalia, deities, and religious concepts which the Santal hold in common. Apart from those important deities that belong exclusively to the various social units (house, local lineage, village, and the multi-village *Pargana*), there are a series of closely associated deities that belong to all the Santal. These deities are worshiped in a variety of contexts but their special abode is the "Sacred Grove" (*Jaher*), a clump of trees,* lying just beyond each village. The Sacred Grove is particularly the residence of *Maran Buru*, a kind of "national spirit of

---

* These trees are left standing during the initial clearing when the village is established. They are largely *Shorea robusta* (*Sarjom*).

the Santal" as Culshaw properly describes him.⁴ Other "nationally" shared deities of the Grove are *Jaherera, Lĩțā, Gõsãe Era* (Hindi: *Gosain* = pious one), *Mõŗeko* (the Five) and *Tureko* (the Six).*

Marań Buru is regarded as a kind of chief deity, though that honor is sometimes ascribed to Cando (literally "moon," as in Hindi, *chand*) or Sin-Cando (sun-moon) to Thakur, etc. The great variety of names associated almost haphazardly with the notion of "chief" or "biggest" deity is consistent with the acephalous Santal social structure. Nevertheless the Santal do manifest tribal solidarity, and though every house, local lineage, etc., has its own deities, Marań Buru always receives his portion of sacrifices, gift offerings and prayer. This constitutes another link between the Santal and other Mundari tribes of the region, who share most of these deities.

Sinha has characterized Indian tribals as conceiving of the good life as one with "ample scope for indulgence in pleasure, while maintaining social obligations to corporate group or groups" (Sinha 1959:309). Culshaw similarly begins his chapter on "Dancing, Music, and Poetry" with the comment that the word "*ŗaska* meaning 'pleasure' is often on the lips of the Santal, and it is dear to their hearts."⁵ One could hardly begin such a chapter differently, for the traditional sense of the word "pleasure" (*ŗaska*) makes it virtually synonymous with dancing

---

⁴ Culshaw, *ibid.*

* *Jaherera* is sometimes called *Jaher Buḍhi* ("Old Lady of the Sacred Grove") and is said to be the consort of Marań Buru. *Lĩțā* is prominent in hunting rites; the rainbow is referred to as the "bow of *Lĩțā.*" As for the Five and Six, not even the most erudite of the Santal seem to have any knowledge of them other than when they are to receive offerings and prayer.

⁵ Culshaw, *ibid.*, 39.

and singing, playing and listening to music, eating festively, drinking rice beer, and implicitly sexual activity; in practice, these are the activities characteristic of a Santal festival. When a traditional and typically uneducated Santal meets another from a distant region, one of the first questions asked will be, "How is pleasure in your region?" The reply will focus on the activities mentioned above. Indeed, the only occasion in which I observed a fully sober Santal male adult burst into tears was during such a festive event. When I asked the old man why he was weeping at such a time, he replied, "The sounds of the drum remind me of the pleasure of my youth and of my deceased wife who shared in my pleasure." It will be recalled that it was rice beer which enabled the propagation of the Santal to proceed in the beginning of things, and if there is one word which is more frequently uttered than any other, more frequent even than the sound of festive drums, it is the cry of *"haṇḍi, haṇḍi haṇḍi"* (rice beer; from *handia,* Hindi = an earthenware container). As the Santal sing:

> Oh "flower friend"*
> I am thirsty and I am hungry;
> But hearing the sound of the drums under the canopy†
> My thirst and hunger are banished.

The Santal pleasure complex is of primary importance in considering recent economic and political events, but here the concern is with "pleasure" as a shared understanding serving the solidarity of the Santal. As the Santal think of it, "pleasure"

---

* A "flower friend" or *phul* (as in Hindi *phul* = flower) is a formally celebrated ritual friendship.

† The "canopy" or *chamda* is utilized in wedding ceremonies to cover the area in which the ceremony takes place.

is pre-eminently a social phenomenon: it obtains essentially during festivals, which are community events; it derives from a festive atmosphere, which only the assembled community can create; and it reaches its community-centered peak as throngs of men and women form a large dancing circle, men and women alternating so that each one has a member of the opposite sex on each side, hands joined together. While I am sensible of anthropological naïveté, the remarks and demeanor of the Santal on such occasions leave little doubt that such performances are a potent source as well as a reflection of community solidarity. During and just after such dancing there is generally great camaraderie, and everyone exchanges cigarettes and rice beer while moving about from one house to another.

Although it is above all village solidarity which such festivals enhance and reflect, they also draw together the members of a particular village and Santal from as far as thirty miles away. The Santal are aware of the attraction of the drums and in many regions festivals are celebrated at slightly different times by nearby villages so that one can participate in several, and so that reciprocity becomes possible. "Pleasure," as the Santal understand the term, is a shared understanding which creates immediate bonds with co-tribals wherever they may be from, and, like many other more official boundary-marking symbols of solidarity, also binds the Santal to the neighboring Mundari tribes; it is not uncommon to find some members of several of these tribes participating in any particular Santal festival. To be sure it is also possible to see drunken men quarreling at a Santal festival, and other signs of discord, but this will be discussed later.

The Santal origin myth validates the kinship ties between all Santal and thereby provides a basis for such unity as the Santal

9

have achieved. For the traditional Santal, membership in the tribe constitutes the widest bond of social identification. This is true even though as far back as historical records extend (to the early nineteenth century), the Santal have not been politically unified. Beneath the level of the somewhat nebulous tribe there are interpenetrating territorial and kinship organizations. Territorially, the largest formally organized unit is the *Pargana* (Hindi = a subdivision of a district), a loose confederation of approximately a dozen villages bound together to settle certain judicial questions. Its proceedings are conducted by a "Chief" (*Parganath* in Bengali or *Desh-Pradhān* in Hindi). The village (*ato*) is the only other formally organized territorial unit and is often divided into sections (*tola* in Hindi). Village "Chiefs" are known as *Mañjhi* or *Pradhān* (Hindi = Headman); other village officials include an "Assistant Chief" or "Chiefs" (*Jog-mañjhi*) and a "Village Priest" (*Naeke*).

The widest separate kinship unit is the "Clan" (*Paris:* or *Jāti*,* Hindi = Caste). According to the Santal creation myth there should be twelve clans; in fact there appear to be only nine. Clan membership, like all inheritance, is determined patrilineally. Containing thousands of members, the clan is, of course, a fictitious kinship unit; apart from bearing a name and the presumption of some common rituals performed by its constituent local lineages, the clan has few "likenesses" to bind it together and does not exist as a corporate unit. The clan is, nonetheless, an exogamous social entity which serves as a reference point establishing kinship relations among all Santal. Santal unable to trace "actual" common relatives can establish their kin relationship via the clan; for example, a non-kin of the same sex and same clan might be regarded as a brother,

---

* *Jāti* is also used by the Santal to refer to the tribe as a unit.

or an older man of one's mother's clan might be regarded as mother's brother.

The kinship groups within the clan are the sub-clan,* the local lineage, and the extended family, all of which are patrilineal. Each of the many sub-clans within a clan bears a distinctive name, and marriage within the sub-clan is even more severely punished than marriage within the clan. While smaller than the clan it also has thousands of members and is perforce a fictitious kinship group, though on occasion many members within a range of several hundred square miles will assemble for a sub-clan ceremony. The local lineage is a group of patrilineal male kinsmen living within a few miles of one another, periodically worshiping as a unit, and gathering together on such occasions as marriages and funerals. It is the largest corporate group within the kinship system. The patrilineal, patrilocal extended family is a distinctive economic and ritual social unit which often occupies a single house-site, though common residence and economic unity seldom are maintained after the death of the father of the family or the marriage of all of his sons. The nuclear families which together compose the extended family are, as elsewhere, distinguishable units and provide the lines of fracture by which the extended family divides itself.

---

* In the literature the sub-clans are referred to as *khūt*, but I found that throughout the territory of the southern Santal there is no such term; in fact, there is no word which designates "sub-clan." To find out which sub-clan a Santal belongs to, it is necessary first to determine his clan and then to place the interrogative "what" (*cili*) before the name of his clan, e.g., *cili Hansdak*! Casual inquiry among the northern Santal indicates that the same condition prevails there. It is possible that the word *khūt* is a mistranscription of *khond*, which refers to the ceremonial circles which Santal draw and indirectly to the local lineage; in this usage one refers to those who worship "at a single circle" (*mit khondren*). But it is not possible to ask a Santal, "What *khond* do you belong to?"

All interaction among Santal is in part regulated by kinship. For a traditional Santal, it is really impossible to establish a relationship of any depth except on the firm bedrock of kinship. Even the queer saheb anthropologist had to be incorporated into the system and make the utmost effort to maintain properly his ramified kinship relations, including ceremonial greetings, joking, and avoidance relations.

While incorporation into the system is possible, as in the case of an anthropologist or a member of some other caste, it is not the same as with a Santal. No outsider can attain clan membership or affiliation with a local lineage, and there remains an obvious difference between the "fictitious" kinship ties among Santal and those among Santal and outsiders. Indeed, sometimes ties between Santal involving rather close relationships, as among "fictitious" brothers, especially if they are enduring, are difficult to distinguish from relations among actual brothers. In such cases the fictitious brother, originally from some other village or region, may be incorporated into the local lineage of his "brothers," provided that he belongs to the same sub-clan as well; the Santal maintain that the rituals within the various local lineages belonging to a common sub-clan are identical, though in fact they vary considerably.

Thus while the clan, like the tribe, is both acephalous and non-corporate, it actively serves to maintain and structure the ties of kinship which exist among all Santal. Furthermore, as the most extended of patrilinear kin groupings, and as the ultimately exogamous unit, the clans are necessarily interdependent and thereby contribute to the numerous affinal ties binding together their constituent social units.

While it is unclear from accounts of the northern Santal just who it is that participates in the ceremonial functions assigned to the sub-clan, one may presume that the large size of the typical sub-clan and its necessary dispersion prevent the assembling of anything more than a very limited part of its membership. This is certainly the case among the southern Santal, though I have been told that on a few occasions members of a sub-clan have assembled within a territory as broad as the whole district of Mayurbhanj. But such meetings are difficult to arrange and so costly that they cannot be frequent.

The named sub-clan, like the clan, serves to orient kin relations, and as mentioned, enables strangers to be taken into the bosom of a functioning local lineage. It is also the exogamous unit par excellence, i.e., marriage within the sub-clan is unthinkable incest while marriage within the clan, though it is forbidden and usually punished, is a much less serious offense. This difference reflects the much larger size of the clan, the relative weakness of its internal connections, and the lack of "likenesses" within its far-flung organization.

But it is the local lineage which has a truly corporate character, though this corporateness is largely confined to ceremonial activity. The members of this unit share common "house deities" (*orak' boṅga* = house deity) and ancestral spirits, and they celebrate these together at about two- to six-year intervals. These celebrations, in which all male members of the local lineage join together, are held in fields and known as "field worship" (*thandi boṅga* = field deity). Each local lineage has its own distinctive ritual practices, and these practices tend to be kept in considerable secrecy, often being held in fields remote from any village and at hours when villagers are likely to be asleep. Some lineages maintain that anyone viewing their ritual offerings at "field worship" will be stricken ill and die. Still, a number of local lineages invite a few non-lineage members

13

to participate in a prescribed way in this ceremony; in particular they are often asked to become "possessed" (*rum*) and represent either the spirits of the ancestors and/or Maran Buru, the chief deity of the Santal. It is these spirits, representing as they do the unity of the Santal and the local lineage respectively, that must give their approval of the food and other offerings presented to them by the lineage. Non-members thus serve as properly objective outsiders in making this judgment, even though it is done in a state of "possession" in which they are the vehicles of the deity and spirits. It is interesting that these outsiders are frequently mother's brothers or other relatives of a woman married into the lineage; in this way the affinal connections of the local lineage are also given recognition in this ceremony.

The expressions of the Santal regarding this rite indicate that feelings of strength and bravery within the solidary lineage are closely associated with the rites performed. As one Santal put it, "Field worship is of hero Gods; by worshipping them, courage and bravery are gained by the members of the sublineage." Another Santal added, "Nowadays there is no warfare, but these deities are true as anything"; a third then related a famous tale of two Santal heroes who were of his sub-clan.

"Field worship" is inextricably intertwined with certain funerary rites (*bhandan*; Hindi: *Bhāndạ* = an earthen vessel) which are prerequisites for both "field worship" and marriage rites. Representatives of the local lineage must perform the *bhandạn* after the death of any member. Among the northern Santal these rites are generally performed at the Damodar River; some of the southern Santal also journey to the Damodar

but others perform the rites at less distant streams. The fact
that the southern Santal often journey northward to the Damodar for funerary purposes suggests that many of them might
have come from this region southward, bringing the tradition
of the sacred Damodar with them. It is possible that this voy-
aging is either the result of recent contact with the northern
Santal or consultation with the ethnographic literature about
them; however, this seems unlikely since there is no particular
reason why they should have chosen to borrow such an incon-
venient practice from their northern co-tribals. Formerly the
southern Santal deposited certain bones of the deceased at the
river after performing various rites at some Hindu cremation
grounds on the bank of the river. Today, a few coins are
deposited in lieu of bones.*

Before the voyage to the river, members of the local lineage,
together with their wives and other affinal relatives and fellow
villagers of the deceased, join in rites performed within the
deceased's village. However, the local lineage is responsible for
supplying to the spirit of the deceased the offerings which must
be accepted by his spirit as manifested in a medium. The considerable cost involved in supplying these offerings is not totally
lost, since the local lineage customarily sells these offerings
after returning from the river. The arrangements for this procedure represent a compromise which reveals the antagonism
between solidarity and the higgling and haggling of the
market. It is required that the items offered be exchanged at
far less than their cost, that there be no bargaining, and that
members of the local lineage, and in principle even fellow clan

---

* For a relatively complete account of funerary rites, see Culshaw 1949:
Chap. 12.

members, may not purchase them. Thus there is a proper sacrifice, haggling is not allowed to sully the offering, and still all is not totally lost.

Several deaths may accumulate within a lineage before the collection of offerings and voyage to the river are accomplished, and within this period the local lineage may not enter into marriage alliances or carry on "field worship." It is a question of ridding the local lineage of pollution so that the members may re-enter the social life of the community. Voyages to the river are performed during several prescribed periods of the year, and members of several lineages living within a region may journey there together, especially if it is a long voyage to the Damodar.

The eminently social nature of death, for both the deceased and the living, and its interconnection with marriage, lineage solidarity, and social identity are recognized implicitly by the Santal. Thus their very great fear of living exclusively among non-Santal is often expressed by saying, "If we live among others, who will there be to bury us?"

Besides ritual ties, the local lineage, though by no means economically corporate, is a source of mutual aid. To deny food and lodging to members of one's local lineage, while not strictly speaking unthinkable, would be the greatest of social offenses, and if adequate food and lodging are available, something that no sane Santal would contemplate. Indeed, in the absence of shortage—and sometimes even then—to provide generous hospitality to all Santal, i.e., all "kinsmen" (*peṛa hoṛ*) in the most extended sense, is a cause for joy. Generally, when "kinsmen" visit, the man of the house will meet them and cry out to his wife that "kinsmen" have come; the wife brings water, oil (which she rubs on their tired feet), and rice beer if there is

16

any, and then begins to prepare a meal. Within the local lineage these visits are frequent, especially during festivals.

Rice and money are borrowed—always without interest—within the local lineage, though there are cases in which help is denied. Occasionally members may contribute funds so that a young member may obtain an education; however, prior to this century education was extremely rare among the southern Santal, among whom missionary efforts were not nearly so intense as among the northern Santal.

Though an entire local lineage is not likely to reside in a single village, the members inevitably live near one another. Typically, the founders of a village are members of a single local lineage. Members of this founding lineage thus tend to have more and superior land than later immigrants. In most instances the chief offices of the village, i.e., "village headman" and "village priest" belong to the founding lineage. The rule of primogeniture obtains, though upon the death of any officer the villagers must accede in the choice of a new officer. To what degree the villagers may in fact determine who shall fill the position is not clear, though there are cases in which an older son of a deceased headman or priest was passed over in favor of a younger son on the basis of alleged incompetence. Although the village must give its assent in selecting leaders—and to the decisions of leaders as well, since there is nothing more than the consent of the governed to support such decisions—important control of village affairs does lie within the control of the founding local lineage through its control of offices, superior wealth, and prestige.

In the traditional system, disputes within a village are brought to the attention of the headman by the contending parties. He may suggest some compromise if it is not a question of serious concern to the entire village. If his suggestion is not accepted, or if the matter is of village concern, he may call together the so-called "Five People" (*mõre hoṛ*). The "Five People," obviously homologous with the Hindu *Panchayāt*, actually consist of as many married males from the village as wish to participate. After prolonged discussion, the headman will pronounce what he takes to be the general consensus and will ask if this is not acceptable. According to the traditional way of stating the matter, "all must agree" for a decision to be reached, but this requirement does not quite mean that all must be convinced that the decision is a good one.

To understand the nature of this consensus, which is an important element in Santal solidarity, one must consider the relation between morality and solidarity in the Santal view. For the traditional Santal, what the "people" say is good and true *is* good and true. Like other peoples, the Santal are not entirely consistent in this matter, but they do regard consensus as the basis of morality. Though the facts of any particular issue must be decided upon the basis of evidence presented, true moral rules are felt to lie in the matrix of the traditional cultural heritage. Thus, when it is a question of deciding what the rules are or ought to be, the "people" ostensibly consult the unwritten records of their tradition.

The Santal are well practiced in giving assent to what appears to be consensus. Thus it is quite proper to move from the minority to the majority viewpoint not because one ought to be accommodating or because one has seen the light, but rather because the voice of the people is the voice of tradition—and since the traditional is sacred, it would not be far wrong to say the voice of the sacred as well.

The practice of readily giving assent to prevailing views

18

which are held to be traditional, sacred, and true is a necessary characteristic of a society where leaders voice consensus rather than promulgate edicts and where there is no specialized police force. Perhaps the Santal are as "tradition-directed" as a society may be. This means that weight is given to tradition in making decisions, but it does not mean, as abundant evidence soon to be presented will indicate, that Santal culture is static. It means rather that the "people," like our Supreme Court, must justify their decisions in terms of real or alleged traditional precepts and practices. As our own historical experience indicates, tradition so interpreted and utilized allows for considerable flexibility. Thus it would probably be more accurate to call Santal society (and possibly other societies known for reverence of the traditional) "tradition-justifying," rather than "tradition-directed."

The dominance of a particular local lineage in a village is joined with village solidarity, just as the officials of the village are recruited from this lineage. Every village has its "headman's shrine" (*mañjhithan*) ; here as at the "Sacred Grove" the deities are represented by unworked stones. The central deity of this shrine is "Oldman Headman" (*Mañjhi-Haṛam*), who is the spirit of the founding father of the village, i.e., the first headman. At various ceremonies the headman or priest, accompanied by the villagers, makes offerings to Oldman Headman, who is, of course, of their lineage. By contributions to the offerings to Oldman Headman and by various formal and informal gestures, the villagers both acknowledge the authority of their village officials and participate in commemoration of village solidarity.

In some contexts village membership and solidarity are paramount. Fellow villagers must worship together on prescribed

19

occasions, bury or cremate one another, assist each other during illness or scarcity, entertain one another, and make "pleasure" possible. They may hunt together, jointly stock some pool with fish and generally carry on the daily routine of work and leisure side by side. Santal kinship groups are important within the village, but they are not nearly so divisive as Hindu castes. Neither the clan, the sub-clan, nor the local lineage is endogamous nor so structured as to limit social relations with non-members. Indeed, all are exogamous and it is only the entire tribe which in some respects is equivalent to a Hindu caste. The Santal village is therefore more internally solidary than a Hindu village of the region, though many clans may be represented.

Though not formally so, the village is in practice almost completely exogamous. This is partially due to the close relations between villagers and to the feeling that if a man's in-laws, and particularly his brothers-in-law, are living in his village, he will have difficulty in "disciplining" his wife; to put it as the Santals do, "She will run home to her house all the time making trouble between her husband and her brothers."

The tie to one's village is also supported by the attachment to the agricultural land which generally surrounds the few rows of houses and which is regarded as an integral part of the village. Besides the founding spirit of the village there are distinctive "boundary deities" (*sima bonga*) marking the special attachment to one's own village.

As indicated earlier, the village is tied to about a dozen nearby villages in a quasi-judicial relationship. The head of this confederation is in many respects a multi-village headman. He is generally recruited from that local lineage which first migrated to the area; his tenure and appointment are subject to the approval of the villagers with whom he is associated; he presides generally at disputes which cannot be settled within a particular village, at inter-village disputes or at discussions of custom which are of concern to the entire set of villages under his jurisdiction; like the headman of a village, he is at most *primus inter pares*. Publicly he is little more than the voice of consensus, though privately his influence is that of an especially respected and powerful person.

The "justice" of the Santal, i.e., their institutionalized practices as distinct from the desires of injured parties, places a strong premium on rendering decisions which will restore severed relationships and permit life to return to what it was before the dispute. The fee to the "court" is often as substantial as a judgment and must be paid by both parties. There is almost always encouragement to settle "out of court" by friends and officials. Fees paid to the "court" are generally spent to buy rice beer and viands so that after the bitterness of the contest both court and contestants join together in "pleasure," and all is as it was. These gatherings to settle disputes within the village are usually called "discussions" (*galmarao*) ; multi-village gatherings are known as *dorbar* (Hindi, *dorbar* = court).

Besides the judicial tie, each village is bound to a number of others by marriage. Marriage procedures will be discussed at length but it is appropriate here to note that marriage is arranged with the aid of villagers and village officials as well as those associated by kinship and is of great interest and concern to the whole village. The ceremonies of marriage dramatize this concern, reflecting village solidarity in gaining and accepting a daughter or sorrowfully giving one up, as the case may be.

Beyond the multi-village judicial organization there are no formally organized territorial units: however, regional cultural

21

variation and specialization do exist even though there are few sharp boundary lines. There is one regular social event which reflects and intensifies regional cultural and social interconnection; this event is an annual hunt followed by a large all-male gathering outside some village where performances largely humorous and/or "obscene" (in their eyes as well as mine) take place. The participants consist of teams generally from several villages within a vicinity, and they compete with other similarly constituted teams for the favor of the assembled throng. Like many such gatherings, it terminates with rice beer.

In most of the territory occupied by the southern Santal, game is so scarce that the hunting aspect of this yearly event has become *pro forma*. After the hunt and its rituals, the various teams proceed in a march-dance parade through different villages as they make their way toward the final gathering place where performances will be held. Vigorous drum-beating marks the progress of their procession, and the characteristic Santal male strutting in dance is particularly pronounced. Any game that has been shot is borne aloft on pole stretchers. The entire event is known as *Sendra*.

Several of my informants as well as the literature maintain that serious discussions of Santal customs and even settling of disputes that have escaped solution within the judicial units occur after the hunt. This was not the case at the one *Sendra* I attended. However this may be, the *Sendra* remains the largest and territorially the widest gathering of Santal, sometimes bringing together more than a thousand Santal living within a radius of about fifty miles.

Still to be considered are the intertwined components of the extended and nuclear family. The term "extended family" is unfortunately one which has often been used very loosely; it sometimes refers to three generations occupying a single household with joint control and merging of all income; sometimes income stipulations are disregarded; some speak of the extended family exclusively in terms of joint income, and some regard any three-generational family unit that occasionally gathers together or in which there is some financial cooperation as "extended." It is not always clear which criteria are being applied, and the different uses involve partially independent variables. To avoid possible ambiguity, each of these variables will be discussed separately with appropriate reference to their interconnections.

In the traditional farming situation, Santal living in the same house consist of a patrilineal group of kin plus wives, and income is typically part of a single fund managed officially by the eldest male, i.e., the father, or the eldest brother if the father is deceased. Income goes into the family coffers—whatever its source. However, a young married son living apart may not manage his own income; he might have recently married and had a house built for himself and his new wife while continuing to work his father's or his brother's land. Such arrangements may persist until there is an occasion for a division of the family land among the various members. Santal families tend to remain together as both a household and an economic unit until the death of the father. However, the marriage of a son is frequently sufficient to force a division of the land before the father's death. The Santal always attribute such divisions to the quarrelsome nature of women, as do many other patrilineal peoples. However this may be, the nuclear family begins to emerge as a unit in its own right immediately after marriage and to provide the lines of eventual fracture. In the village of Fanderkuta, less than 15 per cent of the 48 households (i.e., seven) were extended in the sense of consisting of an undivided family of three generations with pooled income. There were also five households in which a mother had moved in with one of her divided married sons. The mere fact that the average life span of the Santal is relatively short and the fact that families generally fracture after the father's death are sufficient to account for the preponderance of the nuclear family.

Each economically undivided family has a part of the house set apart for the purpose of worship and sometimes also for the storing of rice and other valuables. A wall extending nearly across the house divides the largest room of the house in two; it is the smaller portion which is set apart, and it is known as the "inner room" (*bhitạr*; inside, as in Hindi). On almost all festivals, offerings of rice beer are made here to the patrilineal ancestors, accompanied by prayers asking that the family be spared sickness (*hạndi boṅga* = rice beer worship). At this offering the head of the household usually presides, accompanied by one or more male relatives. Offerings may be brought by females of the household if they are not menstruating at the time, but females not of the household may never enter on the grounds that "one never knows their condition." "Rice beer worship," with its offerings to the ancestors, is obviously expressive of the bonds within the extended family, but *Maraṅ Buru*, the tribal deity, also receives his offering during ancestor worship, expressing the unity of the tribe.

Aside from the interconnected strands of kinship and territory, there is another socially relevant characteristic—wealth. As a social marker, like the inheritance of tribal offices, it provides social positions not attainable by all in the normal life process. Much will be said of its divisive effects later; it is appropriate to note here that it operates in establishing mar-

24

riage connections by joining together families of approximately equal wealth and that it is an important source of power. There is a strong tendency for village officers and other members of founding lineages to be richer than later immigrants; hence wealth tends to be joined with hereditary office. In the informal councils which precede formal deliberations over disputes or policy, men listen more attentively to the statements of the wealthy. This attentiveness is a sign of respect, but also of recognition of the wealthy individual's ability to give or withhold favors; sometimes there is also the informal bribery of generous hospitality, and on occasion, outright bribes in return for support. Wealth differences can result in special likenesses and differences within Santal society, and even ceremonies graded in cost, as will be discussed later.

It would normally go without saying that those who hold positions of special power and prestige have a special interest in the preservation of traditional solidarity and provide a natural source of endogenous pressure for the maintenance of traditional structure. It receives mention here only because it will soon be shown that other circumstances make these same privileged Santal especially subject to tribally disintegrative centrifugal pressures.

Chapter 2   External Solidarity

The "likenesses" of a particular people not only contribute to internal bonds of solidarity, but by virtue of their distinctiveness may also serve as a barrier against assimilation in surrounding societies. The more distinctive these likenesses, the more inconsistent with the culture of the surrounding societies, the better they serve to preserve solidarity.

The chief traits which have divided the Santal from their predominantly Hindu neighbors are the "pleasure" complex mentioned earlier and the practices of cow sacrifice and beef eating. Among the practices associated with the pleasure complex the most conspicuous are public mixed dancing such as occurs at festivals and the drinking of rice beer, as well as its ritual use. The Hindus regard Santal mixed dancing as an orgy, although it is in fact no more promiscuous than Western mixed dancing and is certainly less sensuous than much of Hindu classical dancing. As for cow sacrifice and beef eating, the stringency of the Hindu attitude is well known; on many occasions armed force has been used to halt both. It is again significant that these distinctive traits are shared by the other

27

Mundari tribes of the region, for the tribes are thereby bound to one another and set apart from the surrounding Hindu society.

Of course, there are many other distinctive practices which have contributed to external solidarity, two of the more important among them being the language spoken and the deities worshiped. But the Hindus have demonstrated such a genius for incorporating alien cultures and societies that one cannot satisfactorily account for the maintenance of distinctiveness of the Santal and some other closely related tribes of the region on the basis of contrasting likenesses. To begin to understand the preservation of these societies it is necessary to shift to an historical perspective of the social relations between the tribal societies of the region and the increasingly dominant Hindu society.

All about the Santal are examples of formerly Mundari-speaking tribals who have become Hindus. Most conspicuous to the Santal are the Bhumij, numbering over a hundred thousand and living interspersed throughout the territory of the southern Santal. Still bearing Mundari clan names, and some few still speaking a dialect of Mundari, most are nevertheless socially Hindus. According to Sinha, who has done extensive field work among these people, the Bhumij in most regions regard themselves and are regarded by others as Hindus; this is supported by my own observations (Sinha 1956). Like other low castes, they are not often rigorously assigned a particular level in the caste hierarchy, but they do enter into active economic relations with the various Hindu castes of the region. Unlike the Santal, many regard the employment of such Hindu castes as Brahmans, barbers, and washermen as essential, and most speak only the regionally prevailing Indian language, i.e., Bengali, Hindi, or Oriya.[1]

One hears of a Bhumij chief of Barabhum who claimed to be a Rājput Kṣatriya and employed degraded Brahmans. In Manbhum thirty years ago there was a Bhumij Kṣatriya who was a large landlord and who protested against his enumeration in the census as a *Bannya Jai* (Hindi = "wild tribe"); he claimed that his rituals conformed with high-caste Hindu standards. He and his retainers who were served by Brahmans and by members of other Hindu castes regarded themselves as superior to the "unclean" artisan and servant castes but inferior to the priestly Brahman and Boishtom castes. Apparently, there is considerable confusion among the "other" Hindu castes as to the rank of this group of Bhumij. Only twenty years ago the women of these Bhumij joined in public mixed dancing and the men still sacrificed chicken at their Sarhul festival. Nevertheless their Pargana was becoming endogamous and their clans had ceased to be exogamous.

Though Hinduization is general among the Bhumij and other tribals in the area, there is a tendency for those tribals who hold traditional offices and/or those who are wealthy to be more acculturated and assimilated than others.

In some regions occupational specialization has occurred, e.g., the Shelo Bhumij of Dhalbhum who are iron smelters and smithies, and the Shelo Kamar of Manbhum, who are blacksmiths and no longer regard themselves as Bhumij.[2] But the Bhumij are not the only tribe so affected, nor is the process of Hinduization confined to this or even simply the last century.

---

[1] Sinha *ibid*.
[2] Sinha *ibid*.

As early as the sixteenth century a Munda tribal in the Ranchi district established himself as a local Rājā.[3] By virtue of his wealth and power he attracted reputable Brahmans to his court who Sanskritized his rituals and manufactured for him a Rājput genealogy. Eventually this status was accepted by other Rājputs and marriage ties were established.

There are numerous other examples, and the Santal themselves have undergone considerable Hindu acculturation and some fission and Hindu assimilation though not nearly to the same degree or in such large numbers as the Bhumij. Hindu-tribal contact in the region has been long and intense. All the tribes in the area have been heavily influenced by Hindu culture, some have been partially and others totally absorbed in the Hindu social order and no doubt many Hindu castes have been so recruited in instances where the historical record is unknown. Why the Bhumij have been assimilated and the Santal, Munda, Ho, and some others have not must be understood by reference to particular historical differences which are beyond the scope of this investigation. However, the examination of Santal historical experience does shed light on the general conditions which are relevant to assimilation as well as on the specific historical events which were crucial to the Santal experience.

Perhaps the single most important event in the history of Santal-Hindu relations was the Santal rebellion of 1855–57. This major public event, which first drew the serious attention of India's English rulers to the Santal, reveals at once the nature of Santal-Hindu relations and the strengths and limitations of Santal solidarity. Commemorated in Santal songs and

---

[3] Roy 1912.

discussions, it is part of the Santal living cultural heritage and hence of continuing influence.

Various investigations of the rebellion support Man's conclusion that the following four Santal grievances were chiefly responsible for the rebellion: (1) "grasping and rapacious money lenders"; (2) "personal and hereditary debt bondage"; (3) "corruption and extortion by police helping moneylenders"; (4) "impossibility of Santal getting court redress" (Man 1867: from Culshaw and Archer 1945). A fifth contributing factor of an endogenous nature is what Man describes as Santal "improvidence."[4] Leaving aside Man's pejoratives, there is abundant evidence that his understanding of the rebellion was substantially correct. By legal and extra-legal means the Santal were systematically being stripped of their ownership rights over their land and becoming tenants and even slaves of Hindus who knew how to manipulate the law and were accustomed to gaining their ends in the context of the market.

The Santal felt themselves exploited, and not without cause. The emphasis in their culture on "redistribution"[5] and other leveling mechanisms plus their heavy commitment to "pleasure" made the Santal easy prey of the merchant and moneylender. To the British observers and to the Hindus the Santal were "improvident." Ultimately the Santal erupted in a violent revolt during which they mutilated a number of Hindu moneylenders and took vengeance on guilty and innocent alike. One reads of a Hindu money lender whose limbs were severed one

---

[4] See Datta 1940 for the most complete bibliography of relevant primary documents.

[5] Polanyi 1957.

at a time to signify payment of four annas on the rupee, an annual interest rate of twenty-five per cent.[6]

The rebellion was not begun on the spur of the moment as a result of sudden passion. The Santal had made many attempts to present their grievances to the government but were rebuffed for various reasons and by various means. Numerous meetings and communications between Santal villages preceded armed revolt. In spite of the lack of any formal political structure wider than the Pargana, and equipped only with bow and arrow and ax, the Santal were able to overrun all local opposition and even to defeat a crack unit of British-led troops in one skirmish. After intermittent battles lasting over a year the Santal were finally defeated with heavy losses, their rebellious leaders were executed or sent to prison, and the revolt gradually ceased.

Confirmation of official findings and an "inside view" of the rebellion is conveyed by such enduring songs as the following:

> Sido, why are you bathed in blood?
> Kanhu,* why do you cry *hul hul*?†
> For our people we have bathed in blood
> For the merchant thieves have robbed us of our land.[7]

> Saheb rule is trouble full;
> Shall we go or shall we stay?
> Eating, drinking, clothing,
> For everything we are troubled.
> Shall we go or shall we stay?[8]

---

[6] Culshaw and Archer 1945.
* Sido and Kanhu were the two brothers who led the revolt.
† *Hul* = rebellion.
[7] Archer 1945:207.
[8] Culshaw and Archer 1945:218.

Though the Santal demands which preceded the rebellion were limited to relieving their economic plight, the preparations for the rebellion and certain events during its course suggest a more radical intent. For example, two brothers, Sido and Kanhu, proclaimed to their fellow Santal that they had supernaturally received a message to worship *Suba Thakur* (Hindi = Head of a District), presumably a deity associated with the political leadership of a District on the analogy of traditional Santal village and Pargana deities; the brothers claimed that *Suba Thakur* had urged them to lead the Santal people in a rebellion. They announced "We will kill and make an end of all the Deko,* rule ourselves, and whoever does not listen, show him a sword."[9] As the author of a settlement report put it, "A deeper or at any rate a supervening cause [for the rebellion] was the Sonthal yearning for independence, a dream of the ancient days when they had no overlords."[10]

At least those who led the rebellion foresaw in victory not only economic relief but increased political power and an opportunity to improve the rank of the Santal. The goal of rank improvement is suggested by a number of ritual practices emulative of Hindu customs which accompanied the rebellion, such as putting on the sacred thread, ritual use of sun-dried rice and oil and vermilion, and purification with cow dung.[11] While wishing to triumph over the oppressive Hindus, the Santal thought of cashing in on the victory with the traditional Hindu symbols of rank. This ambivalence toward the Hindus is a constant characteristic of Santal-Hindu relations.

---

* *Deko*, or *Diku*, as it is pronounced in the south, is a term of opprobrium for foreigners, particularly Hindus.

[9] Culshaw and Archer 1945:2.

[10] McPherson from Culshaw and Archer, *ibid.*

[11] Culshaw and Archer 1945.

The 1855–57 rebellion had its center in the District of Santal
Pargana and extended westward into Bhagalpur and southeast-
ward into Birbhum, which at the time were districts of Bengal.
Though the rebellion did not directly involve the southern
Santal living in the princely states, songs and stories about it
did filter south. In 1832 a rebellion had occurred further to the
south in the Ranchi District; it probably involved several tribal
peoples, especially the Munda.[12] The southern Santal of Seraikela have a tradition of a rebellion having occurred in the latter
part of the nineteenth century. They and the rest of the southern Santal, including those of Mayurbhanj, tell a story of two
men, sometimes said to be brothers, named Diba and Kisun,
whose exploits parallel those of the northern heroes, Sido and
Kanhu:

> They had such power that within their boundaries no horse could
> pass; they achieved power from the deities; they were from Matkom-
> beda, a village in Seraikela; they fought against the Rājā; they shot
> red-hot arrows; they were finally caught; both were of the Soren
> clan; they were against the government; the government collected
> many kinds of rent and taxes; Diba said, 'My goats were carried
> away by a fox, why does the State not give me compensation; my
> chickens were carried away by a crow, why does the State not give
> me compensation; the State does nothing so why should the people
> pay rent and taxes to the State.'

It is said that the children of Diba are still living, and one old
man of about sixty claimed that Diba was his sister's father-in-
law. Many Parganas are said to have joined the rebellion, but

---

[12] Thornton 1843.

it is difficult to estimate the territory involved from the information I obtained.

Though the rebellions of both the northern and southern Santal were unsuccessful, they did draw attention to the plight of the Santal and thus led to enactment of some partially ameliorative judicial and administrative reforms. At the same time, the Santal must have recognized after these defeats that under prevailing conditions, increased political power and improvement in rank were not to be obtained by military might. Evidence to be presented later suggests that this recognition contributed to a decline in solidarity.

The dream of ancient days of independence, which, as has been seen, antedated the rebellions, is a kind of dream which is continually nourished by the character of Santal-Hindu social relations. Santal mythology of the nineteenth century and the present is replete with allusions to former days of independence and glory. One favorite myth reported in the nineteenth century and still prevalent describes a mighty kingdom which the Santal once constituted. Each clan had a specialized function, like that of a Hindu caste: the Kisku were kings, the Murmu priests, the Soren warriors, etc.[13] The Santal are thus pictured as independent, powerful, and constituted exactly in the image of an ideal Hindu kingdom. Like all current dreams of the past, this myth expresses current interests. It says that "we were once great as the Hindus presently are." Though serving as a charter for present independence and improved rank, like the emulative symbols of the rebellion, it is Hindu greatness which is sought.

According to mythological history, the Santal were continu-

---

[13] Bodding 1942:10.

ally forced to flee the areas where they settled. "As soon as we have cleared the jungle in any country, the Deko come and rob us of it. Still if the Sahabs nowadays did not help them, we should soon drive them to the other side of the Ganges."[14]

A myth concerned with the days before the rebellion refers to the differential emulation of the rich and powerful which has been previously mentioned. It describes the Santal as fleeing from a place called Champa to Saont, where their Rājās adopted Hindu religious practices and set themselves up as Rājputs, intermarrying with a local Rājput family. But according to mythology the people would not follow their converted Rājā and therefore fled to Santal Parganas. Another version of the myth tells of the daughter of a Kisku king who had intercourse with someone of another tribe. The illegitimate child of this union grew up to become the chief advisor of the Kisku king, who sought to arrange a Santal marriage; the Santal people refused, and the king, in anger, threatened to defile all of their daughters by forcibly applying vermilion to their upper forehead and in the central part of their hair—a still acceptable way of obtaining a wife by capture. Rather than submit to such a marriage most of the Santal fled Champa.[15] Thus Santal mythology defends solidarity in the face of the emulation and Hindu social claims of some of its leaders.

Nevertheless, the defeat of the Santal rebellion of 1855–57 appears to have led to increased Hinduization, perhaps in part because the path to higher rank through military force seemed closed. Soon after the rebellion the Kherwar movement developed among the northern Santal. Those who joined this Hindu-

---

[14] Bodding 1942:10.
[15] Bodding *ibid*.

ized sect adopted a number of critical Hindu symbols of rank, such as wearing the sacred thread. They were said to "regard themselves as socially superior to those who do not wear *suta* (Hindi = sacred thread). The "*janeo dhari* Santal [those who wear the sacréd thread] are reluctant to intermarry or have social intercourse with the non-*janeo dhari* Santal."[16] This sect also adjured meat-eating. A prime motivation for the sect's adoption of such practices must have been to attain higher rank.

Both schisms and solidarity in the period shortly after the rebellion are described by Dalton:

> Santals who are under the example and precept of Bengali Hindus have abjured some practices considered impure by the latter and are called Sat Santal, that is, pure Santal; but there is a national antagonism between them [the Santal] and the Hindus that prevents any close fraternization or communion between the races. They are not over particular about food, but nothing will induce them to eat rice cooked by a Hindu, even a Brahman. Unfortunately, during the famine of 1866 this was not known to us. The cooks who prepared the food distributed at the relief center were all Brahmans and it was supposed that this would suit all classes, but the Santals kept aloof and died rather than eat from the hands so hateful to them.[17]

Dalton has somewhat overdrawn the reluctance of the Santal to fraternize with Hindus, but the event he describes and the tenor of his remarks regarding the hatred and fear that the Santal have of Hindu conform with all other reports.

The simultaneous attraction and resistance to the Hindu world appears in the remarks of a sophisticated northern Santal

---

[16] Majumder 1956:62.
[17] Dalton 1872:214

who in 1871 spoke in words almost identical to those one often hears today among the Santal; he says, "We only watch at Hindu festivals [we should only watch]; but as these festivals do not belong to us, Santal do not act rightly [in] offering to the *bonga* (deities) of other races. On account of this our *bongas* are angry with us; it becomes like the state of having a wife and a co-wife, we are not making anybody satisfied."[18] Regarding specific borrowings from the Hindus, this same Santal says, "From the *Dekos* we have from time to time taken over many festivals; but among these there is only one festival that the whole village celebrates, viz., the Karam." He explains that on this occasion the offerings include certain flowers, sun-dried paddy, a type of grass, oil, and vermilion, i.e., the offerings are typically Hindu. They are presented to the Hindu deities Karmu and Dharmu.

> At other festivals taken from the *Dekos*, only the man who celebrates it, worships, and we go to look at it; we do not worship. At the Durga festival such people offer to Durga, at the Kali festival they offer to Kali, at the Monsa festival they offer to Monsa, at the Chata festival they offer to the Chata bonga, at the Pata festival they offer to Mahadeb and at the Jatra festival they offer to Ransig, the Jatra bonga.[19]

Though the Karam festival was certainly taken from the Hindus, it is not the only Hindu ceremony which the Santal communally celebrate. Various other ceremonies practiced in the nineteenth century and today are similar to Hindu cere-

---

[18] Bodding, 1942:158.
[19] Bodding *ibid.*:158.

monies celebrated at approximately the same time, e.g., Sakrat (Hindi: Sankranti), and Dąsæ (Hindi: Dasserah). However, these ceremonies are celebrated with a number of distinctive Santal practices, including animal sacrifice, worship at the Sacred Grove of Santal deities, etc.

The pattern of Santal-Hindu relations is thus one of Hindu domination and exploitation combined with considerable cultural influence. In the nineteenth century the Santal responded to increased Hindu pressure with a number of revolts which ended in defeat. These defeats must have indicated to the Santal that their position could not be improved by armed force nor by any other political means. Following these defeats acculturation and assimilation increased. At the same time there were attempts to curtail emulation of Hinduism and to combat assimilation, indicating the existence of counter-forces favoring solidarity. The advent of the market, population pressure, and increasing wealth differences among the Santal which developed during the latter part of the nineteenth century significantly affected the processes of acculturation and assimilation.

The Advent of the Market

The spread of the market, British Indian law and British protection led to a greater influx of Hindus into the hitherto sparsely populated Chotanagpur plateau. This Hindu influx plus the general growth of population, both Hindu and tribal, rapidly reduced the amount of unexploited land. The Santal record is full of examples of hiving off and forming new villages, new local lineages, and, no doubt, new sub-clans. The *bustee* of Daredih itself, which is now filled with industrial

39

workers, was founded as an ordinary agricultural village not more than about sixty years ago. But such opportunities decreased throughout the nineteenth and this century. One inevitable result was to increase wealth differences and to make them more permanent.

A major consequence of increased wealth differences has been the strain placed on internal solidarity by "envy" (*hisạ*; Hindi: *hinska*) and even more by fear of "envy." What this term conveys is concealed malicious intent based upon desire for what another possesses. Though Santal society has long been plagued with accusations of witchcraft, the notion that its practice is almost invariably deliberate and that it arises from envy is of modern origin. Though it is recognized that men may be "envious," it is thought that females most often are guilty and that it is only they who practice witchcraft. Fertile grounds for envy, and attendant witchcraft, appeared when wealthy Santal began using their capital to hire other Santal, to loan money, paddy, and seed at interest, to buy forest land, and even in a few cases to invest in various small-scale enterprises. Relations arising from these investments are often strained and a source of resentment. Envy also arises from observation of what wealth procures in terms of traditional Santal pleasures and from its use in settling disputes.

Aside from the exacerbation of "envy," which increased wealth differences produced, the market imposed other, more general strains. It is difficult to square the basic reciprocity of relations in a kin society like that of the Santal with the impersonal and contractual relations of the market. Though the Santal struggle over land with as much ferocity as any peasants, they find it hard to insist on strictly market relations with other commodities, especially if pressed by kinsmen. A few Santal entrepreneurs have gained notoriety by their greed, but more have failed in business from having granted credit and finding it difficult to collect the debt. Traditional Santal are poor at haggling even with non-Santal, though they understand the basic principle of the market and may even be conversant with a variety of devices used to swindle the unsuspecting bargainer. They will rise early to buy at a market before it becomes crowded or to intercept dealers on their way who will sell for less while en route. They are often aware of price differences and will walk several miles to buy at the cheaper and sell at the more expensive market. But the traditional Santal, once at the market, is too eager a buyer, too poor a haggler, and too readily drawn into pleasant social intercourse to hold his own.

Despite envy, traditional Santal society developed something of a *modus vivendi* between rich and poor. At all festivals, at marriages in particular, and in everyday affairs the wealthy are required to validate their status by giving more than others. The wealthy are thus the greatest providers of "pleasure" for the community, and though there is envy as well as respect, considerable healing is accomplished and unity restored at major ceremonies to which the wealthy have contributed much. Also, in the traditional setting, even with wealth differences and the context of the market, the cultural gap between rich and poor tended to be minimal. Fifty years ago the "elite" Santal, i.e., those with wealth and power, were almost totally illiterate; their style of life, judging by what one presently observes among illiterate and unschooled members of the elite, was only trivially different from that of their less well-situated neighbors. In terms of "likeness" the solidarity of the community was not greatly disturbed by wealth differences.

Nonetheless, elite Santal were somewhat more Hinduized

than their poorer fellows. Some managed to attract a coterie of high-caste but often impoverished Hindus. One hears of wealthy Santal who spent considerable sums on such associates during trips to and attendance at Hindu festivals. Some who were village headmen or Parganaths (multi-village headmen) established enduring relations with the Mahārājā or local zemindar of their region. These Santal often were given responsibility for tax collection, in return for which they kept a portion and received grants of land.

The Santal have long followed the practice of establishing among themselves, and with other castes, permanent bonds of a kinship type, which are given public recognition in a "flower" (*phul*; Santali and Hindi =flower) ceremony. In some instances an elite family managed to establish such a tie with a Brahman family while ordinary Santal contracted such relations only with other tribals or Hindus of very low caste. *This contact contributed to differential emulation of Hindu practices.* Some of the traditional elite among the southern Santal abandoned beef-eating and cow sacrifice; some affected the dress of high-caste Hindus; a few demanded an end to "capture marriage" (*itut' bapla*) because they did not wish to have close relations with unwealthy families of low status. Though their success in getting the non-elite to follow their Hinduized practices was limited, a certain degree of culture difference was established, to the detriment of solidarity.

However, as the historical evidence indicates and as any contemporary observer could infer, contact with Hindu society has been long and/or intensive, and that portion of Santal culture shared by all Santal is so marked with Hindu traits that it would be a monumental task to indicate all of them. All Santal call on neighboring Hindus of low caste to deliver babies.

Although the Santal used to do some weaving and pottery-making, they have traditionally obtained almost everything except foodstuffs and a few forest products from neighboring tribal or Hindu peoples. Even the drums and the flutes which are so integrated in the "pleasure" complex are invariably purchased from Hindu specialists. Furthermore, elite borrowings have often become "naturalized," i.e., accepted as Santal and then widely adopted so as to close the gap. Nevertheless, emulation of Hindus did not always go unnoticed and it will be recalled that there is evidence of resistance to such Hinduization.

The many Hindu cognates in this text give some indication of the extent of linguistic borrowing. Only a few Santal kin terms are of non-Indo-European origin, and the system of dyadic relations among kin is very much like that of the Hindus; one of the largest clans, Hansdak', has a name clearly of Indo-European origin (*hans* = duck in Santali and Hindi), but one also notes the syncretism with the non-Indo-European (*dak'* = water in Santali). Even parts of the Rāmāyaṇa are sung in Santali and on occasion the Santal are allowed to enter the tale. Considering the prevalence of "parochialization" and "universalization" in India,[20] it is possible that some of what is common to the two cultures is of Santal origin. But the heavy incorporation of vocabulary clearly of Indo-European origin suggests that the flow was largely from the Hindus to the Santal.

Prior to industrial employment in this century a small cultural gap separated the elite and common Santal. Though there was some differential emulation of Hinduism it was largely of isolated traits which often became naturalized, and the basic "pleasure" orientation of the Santal was hardly altered.

[20] Marriott 1955:211.

2
the migration to industrial employment

Chapter 3   The Rise of Education

The advent of the market and the failure of the Santal rebellions to achieve significant political power led to a decrease in Santal solidarity and thereby contributed to an increase in acculturation and assimilation. This effect, however, was limited so long as there was no major industrial development. But with the rise of Jamshedpur and its associated industry and educational establishments, Santal solidarity seriously declined. A critical factor in this process has been the severance of the Santal from the web of traditional social relationships resulting from migration to industrial employment.

In 1900 almost no southern Santal were literate and perhaps none had received any formal education. By 1957 the situation was markedly changed, and the Tata Iron and Steel Company (TISCO) at Jamshedpur has been the primary source of that change. TISCO has built the schools and motivated the Santal to attend them.

Two of the three colleges within the area occupied by the southern Santal were established by TISCO, one in Jamshedpur and one in Chaibasa, a town in Singhbhum. While the number of schools of all levels has increased throughout this area, Jamshedpur has probably as many high schools as all of Mayur-bhanj District. TISCO has also provided a trade apprentice school, and enough elementary schools so that I heard of no instance in which a child missed schooling because of lack of facilities.

The effect on motivation is perhaps even more significant since the Santal throughout the area are affected by it, whatever educational opportunities prevail. Until the mid-1940's, when certain new political positions became available, the industrial town of Jamshedpur was virtually the only place at which an educated Santal might gain some return proportional to his educational investment. The entire structure of positions and salaries in Jamshedpur's industries, particularly in the relatively highly rationalized TISCO, makes it clear, even to the most unsophisticated, that it is educational attainment which is rewarded. Though the Santal chiefly occupy the lower echelons of factory employment, the literacy figures that I obtained comparing villagers, *bustee* dwellers, and city Santal support the conclusion that Jamshedpur is both motivation and lure for the educated Santal.

LITERACY RATE AMONG ADULT MALES

Village	20%
Bustee	42%
City	88%

Because of the limitations of the sampling method used (see pp. 64–65), these figures are probably not perfectly representative except for the city Santal, who were completely surveyed; but the order of difference is significant. Most of this literacy was obtained before coming to Jamshedpur, so that it is not primarily the result of the education facilities actually created by Jamshedpur.

Many Santal children and young men are being sent by their families to live with kinsmen in the *bustees* or city because of their superior educational institutions. Furthermore, almost all children of Santal workers, even females, get some schooling. A key factor, apart from greater recognition of the economic value of education, is that there are few opportunities for these children to contribute to the family income from employment in the vicinity of Jamshedpur; children of villagers, however, began doing various farming chores even before they reach school age. Santal children in particular are very much aware of this difference. Since the number of Santal employed in Jamshedpur has grown rather steadily, so has the number of children of such workers who receive education.

Unfortunately, there are virtually no public figures showing the extent of the growth of literacy and education among the Santal. The following figures for the years 1924 to 1939, provided by the Education Department of the State of Mayurbhanj, give some idea of the steady growth of school enrollment among tribals during this period; no doubt this was accelerated during the boom war years.

My field inquiries indicate that there were no high school graduates thirty years ago and certainly no college graduates. Today there are few villages without at least one student attending high school, and I have met at least seven high school and three college graduates as well as two "B.A. failed," a special Indian designation which indicates a level of attainment as well as failure.

Education not only importantly determines "life chances" but

49

TABLE 1

NUMBER OF ABORIGINE PUPILS*

Year	Number
1924–25	4,801
1925–26	5,221
1926–27	5,569
1927–28	5,874
1928–29	6,140
1929–30	6,111
1930–31	6,068
1931–32	6,244
1932–33	6,730
1933–34	6,555
1934–35	6,569
1935–36	6,618
1936–37	6,466
1937–38	6,877
1938–39	8,473

is such a potent cultural divider that social relations are generally unintelligible today without knowledge of the education of the participants. In conversation, the Santal constantly differentiate people according to whether they are "educated-literate" (*paraoc*'; Hindi: *parna* = to read) or "ignorant-illiterate" (*murukh*; Hindi = ignorant). Education and literacy not only confer social prestige; they also produce a qualitatively different kind of Hinduization than the casual acceptance of a

---

* (Mukherjea) While it is true that there are other "aborigines" in Mayurbhanj, the Santal are the largest of such groups, and there is no reason to think they have contributed a disproportionately small share to these totals. Unfortunately there are no later figures available, nor are there comparable figures for Singhbhum.

few Hindu traits. It is the depth of change which education may produce that holds such significance for Santal solidarity.

Most schools, particularly beyond the first few classes, are not located in Santal villages or even *bustees* and therefore require attendance out of the social context of the Santal community. High schools and colleges are found only in towns and cities, so that the Santal attending these institutions often have to spend the entire school year in these alien communities. Removed from their own supporting social milieu, Santal students are exposed to Hindu influences; since almost all these schools are dominated by Hindu headmasters and teachers, considerable international-ization of Hindu beliefs, attitudes, and practices occurs.

In the Hindu-dominated schools many Santal have learned not to eat beef; from their schoolmates and instructors they hear that beef eating is degrading, but more than this they ob-serve the abhorrence with which it is regarded. They are also told that beef eating is injurious to health: every Santal student has heard and many believe that "you will become blind if you eat beef during the period of your schooling." However, not every Santal who attends school abandons beef eating perma-nently. Many resume the practice after completing school, and some never abandon it. While some of the old, uneducated elite also learned not to eat beef, the internalization of the Hindu prohibition which is achieved in school tends to be more pro-found: internalization leads to wholesale Hinduization rather than the piecemeal adoption of isolated Hindu practices. In general, the longer the schooling, the more profound the in-ternalization. Prior to the 1940's one might have expressed this relationship behaviorally by saying that the probability, e.g., of re-adopting beef eating declines with schooling, but in these days, as shall be shown, new forces have reversed matters be-

51

haviorally. A Santal student with only a few years of schooling may have learned the rank value of a given practice such as beef eating, but may not have internalized the appropriate feeling of repugnance. He will therefore eat beef and drink rice beer on the sly, but prefer to be known as an abstainer.

The "pleasure" traits and the "pleasure" orientation, as well as cow-sacrifice and beef eating, are not only part of the cultural basis of external solidarity; they are also key attributes of low rank value in the prevailing caste system. In the schools one learns, with varying force, that the dominant and powerful Hindus regard both the orientation and the traits associated with it as abhorrent and as symbols of low status. With a high school education or more, internalization is usually adequate to provide Santal with their own abhorrence of this orientation. Such Santal, particularly if they do not return to their native villages but take up residence in Jamshedpur, find themselves unable to participate in the traditional "pleasure" activities, even when they return to or visit a village or *bustee*.

What replaces the "pleasure" orientation is an increased commitment to rank improvement, adequate knowledge of the rank attributes of the Hindu world, and, in the case of the relatively well-educated Santal, the necessary internalization to display these attributes consistently and adequately. As the Santal commonly say, "The 'ignorant-illiterate' do not know who is big and who is small!"

Increased education resulting from the existence and practice of industrial employment has thus widened the cultural gap between the Santal and thereby weakened Santal solidarity. Many uneducated Santal are barely able to interact with the educated and highly acculturated. As one Santal remarked when faced with the prospect of such interaction, "I cannot go to his

house, he is like a *Diku*; before him I feel like a black Santal."
I have heard other Santal remark that they could not sing or
talk freely before a certain educated Santal who was a village
leader because his bearing made them ill at ease. It seems particularly difficult to carry on the normal "pleasure" activities
such as dancing, singing, drinking, and even convivial conversation, before such august Santal. The same gap seen from the
vantage point of the educated is expressed in the following
remarks of an educated woman:

> I am happy now to be living in the city because both my child
> and I were sick from "envy" [i.e., being "envied" by others] when
> we lived in the *bustee*; all are healthy here. I never danced or
> sang in the village though I liked to watch; my mother and sister
> danced but I didn't. When very young I did, but after I started
> going to school, I didn't. Some don't send their children to school
> because others will have "envy" and say that highly educated girls
> will be outcasted for marrying into other castes; that is not true.
> Why shouldn't we study as high as money allows? *Diku* girls do.

Less eloquent educated Santal simply explain matters by saying
that they have become "embarrassed" (*lajao*) to dance, sing,
etc.

If differential Hinduization is the major component of the
gap created by education, it is not the only component. An
additional divisive effect of education is that it gives the student
a secular orientation which is highly differentiating but of limited effect since only those with college educations acquire it
thoroughly. There are various manifestations of this orientation, but a particularly interesting example which I have
discussed elsewhere[1] concerns differences in beliefs about witch-

---

[1] Orans 1959.

craft in village, *bustee*, and city. There is increasing secularization of witchcraft belief from village to city, with the *bustee* occupying something of an intermediate position. Among the *bustee* Santal, some are skeptical about the existence of witches, or at least claim to be; I reported such remarks as "Yes, I have seen lights from what are said to be witches, but who knows if they really were? I have never seen a witch myself although others say that they have. Since I have not seen for myself, how can I say whether or not they exist?" Many city Santal argued that witchcraft was not properly speaking a supernatural phenomenon at all but a kind of magical technique, only seemingly supernatural, and referred to it appropriately enough as "mesmerism." A few city Santal positively denied the existence of witchcraft, calling it a superstition of the "ignorant." One student in the Jamshedpur Cooperative College gave a totally naturalistic explanation. In the course of his studies he had read a psychology book which said that people frequently imagine that they see things that they are very much afraid of. He accepted this as a convincing explanation of witchcraft congenial to his acquired secular outlook.

In an earlier interpretation of these differences in belief I gave too much credit to mere residence in the environs of Jamshedpur and the cultural contacts it entailed. Later in my field work I encountered views among the highly educated villagers which were not different than those of the city Santal. I did note, even at the time, that there were no signs of such secularism among the father or the Santal neighbors of the Jamshedpur Cooperative College student mentioned above; indeed, these uneducated Santal found the psychological explanation quite unconvincing. Examination of background material on those city Santal having a secular view of witchcraft indicates that almost all were exceptionally well-educated. The differences between village, *bustee*, and city Santal in witchcraft belief are statistical, reflecting the differences in education between the members of these three kinds of communities.

Increased education is significant for the solidarity of the Santal since it is not equally distributed among them. Generally, it widens the gap between the Santal who are already wealthier and occupy prestigeful hereditary positions and the mass of Santal without wealth or position. This differential distribution of education results from its cost; there are the direct expenses for tuition and books and living expenses away from home, plus the sacrifice of labor which farm families in particular must make in sending their children to school. The cultural gap furthers the social gap. As indicated, the educated and traditional elite are "envied" and fearful of "envy"; in spite of the secular explanations given of witchcraft, many Santal working and living in Jamshedpur are reluctant to return to their villages for fear of witchcraft and the "envy" which is held to motivate it. The same fear prompts the powerful and wealthy who have children attending school to keep those children out of their native village, lest their presence arouse "envy."

Besides straining internal relations by accentuating divisive tendencies already present, by increasing Hinduization education reduces the differences between Santal and Hindu and thereby threatens the external aspect of solidarity. The very orientation and practices which served so well to separate the Santal from the Hindu are simultaneously the attributes of low status in the prevailing system of caste ranking. To maintain these practices which serve solidarity so well is to forego the

55

opportunities of rank improvement through emulation of high Hindu practices. To abandon these practices is to weaken solidarity. The ambivalence which this situation arouses, and which continually manifests itself in the course of Santal-Hindu relations, shall be referred to as the "emulation-solidarity conflict." Increased education resulting from industrial development and employment may then be said to have increased emulation of Hinduism and decreased Santal solidarity.

Chapter 4   The Decline of Ceremonies

The historical works of Max Weber and the anthropological studies of Manning Nash both point up the significance of migration to industrial employment. Weber argued "that the simple fact of a change of residence is among the most effective means of intensifying labor. . . . The simple fact of working in quite different surroundings from those to which one is accustomed breaks through the tradition and is the educative force." Weber notes "how much of American economic development is the result of such factors"; similarly, he calls attention to the Jewish Babylonian exile and the migration of the Parsees to India.[1] Weber thought this change-of-scenery effect to be even more significant than new cultural contacts.

Nash's Guatemalan study confirms the significance of migration by demonstrating how little social and cultural change there may be where there is industrial employment without migration.[2] Taking Africa as his example, Nash notes that particularly "where the effects of industrialization upon [African]

[1] Weber 1958:191.
[2] Nash 1958.

tribal peoples has been most marked, special circumstances attend the disruptions. In most of Africa, money wages and industrial work have been accompanied by the separation of the wage worker from his village, with his consequent removal from the sanctions and social controls of the tribal society."[3]

The pronounced cultural and social changes observed among the Santal should add to the evidence indicating the significance of migration. In addition the microscopic form of anthropological inquiry used with the Santal reveals something more of the *modus operandi* of migration to industrial employment than can be seen at the macroscopic level at which Weber operated.

Traditional Marriage Forms

The Santal have a number of legitimate or quasi-legitimate forms of marriage. It is the manner in which a marriage is contracted, i.e., whether or not it is arranged, and the way in which it is celebrated, which define the form. The various forms are graded by cost and elaboration of the ceremonies performed, and differ significantly in the ceremonial content. There are relatively few arranged marriages among Santal industrial workers living in *bustees* as compared to those among the Santal living in their traditional native villages. The results of my research into this difference indicate that it is the result of migration to industrial employment, that the shift to unarranged marriages among the workers is the result of weakened bonds with both kin and villages, and finally that this is the result of neither migration nor industrial employment singly, but rather of the two together.

The marriage form with the highest prestige and involving the greatest expenditure is known as *duạr itut' sindur* ("placing

---

[3] Nash 1958:113.

vermilion on the bride at the door"), *duąr bapla* ("door marriage"), or *Diku bapla* ("Hindu marriage"); henceforth it shall be referred to as *DB*. All these names call attention to the fact that in this form, as distinct from all others, vermilion is applied to the bride before the door of the bride's house rather than the groom's. The term *Diku bapla* reminds one in addition that application of vermilion at the bride's house is the Hindu custom, while in all other forms of marriage it is applied at the groom's house. It also points to the fact that this form generally involves more Hindu traits than any other. Unlike the other forms, a proper *DB* requires the hiring of a Hindu band and dancers, and the performance, before the application of vermilion, of the marriage of the bride to a tree, a rite which is practiced by many neighboring Hindu castes. The *DB*, like other arranged marriages, allows the couple if they are mature to give or withhold consent before marriage arrangements are completed. Such consent is almost always forthcoming, for a Santal girl rarely dares to go against her parents' wishes. Nearly all the inhabitants of both the bride's and groom's village are involved in the marriage ceremony and ensuing activities. A large party from the groom's village accompanies the groom to the village of his bride. Tradition requires his family to hire from some Hindu caste (usually Harijans or members of other castes of low status) a number of men to carry the groom on a palanquin to the bride's house; a Hindu dancing girl and entertainers ought also to be part of the entourage. Today, if the groom happens to be a TISCO worker returning to his village to have a *DB* marriage, he may be borne by a hired taxi instead. One such worker imported for the occasion, a hired wagon equipped with a phonograph and loud speakers, thereby enabling his rural brethren to listen to Indian cinema music in which the syncopations of "rock 'n roll" were considerably in evidence.

The large number of participants in a *DB* not only gives testimony to affluence of the families being united but is indicative that the marriage establishes a bond between villages as well as between kin and the couple. This broader social implication is borne out by certain obligatory acts in all marriage forms but is particularly conspicuous in the two highest forms. In both of these forms the concern of the entire village is most dramatically expressed in two rites which precede the marriage, i.e., the "scold the husband song" (*jawǣ eger sereṅ*) and the "riddle song" (*episet' seren'*). The first of these rites, which is performed in the bride's village before the marriage rite itself, involves mocking the appearance, virtue, and wealth of the groom and his party and is done by the assembled village females. The second rite is led by a collection of village representatives (*mõṛe hoṛ*) which may include any of the married men of the bride's village. They halt the groom's party along the pathway to the bride's house demanding answers to riddles. It is made to appear that the groom's party shall not be permitted to pass if the correct answers are not forthcoming. On one occasion which I observed, the correct answers were not given, so that the groom's party could only move on by the grace of the village representatives and after being somewhat humiliated. It would appear that the type of riddles posed could not be divined without prior instruction in certain traditional knowledge. One hears such riddles as the following: "What is it that tied walks and untied sits and rests?" Answer: "When you plow, then you tie the bullocks, and you tie the plow to the yoke; if you tie them they will walk and you will chase them; when you finish, you untie them, bullocks and yoke." Or to give another of a more esoteric sort: "It is made of brick and gold-plated. The 'assistant headman' [*Jogmañjhi*] wants a dhoti [a traditional male garb consisting of a rectangular piece of cloth tied about the body in a variety of ways] to be given to the go-between [*raebar*] for a marriage but the 'headman' [*mañjhi*] does not want it to be given." Answer: "This would be during an eclipse (brick and gold-plated). The 'assistant headman' would ask for the dhoti for the go-between, but the 'headman' knows about the eclipse and says no because during an eclipse no marriage can be performed." The significance of this answer lies, of course, in the superior traditional knowledge and authority of the headman.

Each time the groom's party is halted the village representatives make such remarks as "Yes, you must be put to some trouble, for you are taking a bride from us"; or "The oldest son of so-and-so has come to be married but the path is too narrow." With a lack of social understanding which perhaps can only be acquired in college, a "B.A. failed" with a bride's party at one such occasion asked with an appropriately insulting tone what the largest flower in the world was; after rejecting various witty replies, he announced that all present were fools and if they were not all so "ignorant" they would know that it was "rafflesia"!

Members of the groom's party proceed with exaggerated boasts of the great wealth they are bringing. In this and a number of other ways the involvement of the entire village of the bride and that of the groom is expressed. While this is particularly true of the two highest forms of marriage, it is true to some extent even of the lesser forms which require at least the notification of the headman.

The bride-price proper (*gonoñ*) in all forms of Santal mar-

61

riage is fixed at two cows if the bride's father is living, and one if he is dead. Additional payments made by the groom's guardians include the presentation of dhotis to the bride's guardians and to a number of her co-villagers; the cost of these gifts is not fixed but will be greater in a *DB* than in any other form of marriage. The really heavy costs, however, stem from the necessity of transporting and feeding the large party which accompanies the groom's party to the bride's village, hiring the palanquin-bearers or taxi, as the case may be, and providing rice beer for all one's own villagers as well as food for many visitors and relatives from other villages. In a *DB* the groom's guardians may invite a few Hindu acquaintances, whose presence would enhance their Santal host's prestige. Hindus are seldom invited to other forms except occasionally to the second highest form. The total cost of a *DB* in 1957 was Rs. 800–1,500, or, at the going price for rice, 3,200–6,000 lbs.

That the highest, most expensive, and socially most exclusive form (*DB*) tends to be practiced only by the elite Santal, who are also the most Hinduized, is a reflection of the greater acculturation of the elite; it also reflects the general concession of rank to the Hindus, since all Santal regard the *DB* as the highest form.

The second most expensive and prestigeful form of marriage ceremony is the *saṅge bariat* (*saṅge* = many; *bariat* = groom's party; Hindi: *barat* = groom's party). *SB* suggests by its name that like the *DB* it is an arranged marriage involving important and numerous people who accompany the groom to the village of the bride. In bride-price and other gifts and exchanges, it requires about the same expenditure as a *DB*; but since the number of people invited to partake of food and rice beer in both the groom's and bride's village is not so many as in a *DB*, and since the groom is not borne on a palanquin accompanied by hired singers and dancers, the total cost is considerably reduced. The critical ceremonial difference is that, unlike the Hindu practice of the *DB*, the vermilion is applied in front of the house of the groom. This difference, which holds for all the lesser forms as well, is indicative of the generally less Hinduized ritual of the non-*DB* forms. The total cost of an *SB* is Rs. 200–500, or 800–2,000 lbs. of rice.

The least prestigeful and least expensive of arranged marriages is known as *ṭunki dipil* (*TD*) (*ṭunki* = small basket; *dipil* = carried on the head), "A Small Basket Carried on the Head," or *haṛam baṛiạt*, "A Groom's Party of Old Men." Most Santal say that these two names refer to the same form, but a few insist that the latter is a slightly more elaborate form. For the purpose at hand it will be adequate to treat them as identical. The name "Small Basket Carried on the Head" suggests that the bride's possessions and gifts are so few as to be portable on her head; the name "A Groom's Party of Old Men" suggests that the groom's party consists only of a few old men. A *TD* is simply an attenuated form of *SB*, with vermilion similarly applied at the groom's home. The obligation to pay brideprice is weaker and payment is frequently postponed until long after the marriage ceremony; often the debt is never settled. The total cost of a *TD* is generally Rs. 25–100, or 100–400 lbs. of rice.

In addition to the three forms of arranged marriage, and unlike their Hindu neighbors, the Santal have a legitimate traditional form of unarranged or "love marriage" known as *ñapam bapla* (*NB*), "To Meet or Come Together Marriage," or more simply as *ñapam* "To Meet or Come Together." In practice this form may include public announcement, bride-price, and a

63

small-scale celebration, or all these practices may be dispensed with. If ceremony, bride-price, etc., are included, the form is similar to an attenuated *TD*. Bride-price is often postponed and seldom paid. The cost is Rs. 0–75, or up to 300 lbs. of rice.

There are significant differences in the frequencies of these forms of marriage in the village as compared with the *bustee*. The samples drawn were often smaller than necessary to definitively establish conclusions; the sampling was done primarily to serve as a check on previously uncounted impressions. The results bore out those impressions, though in one case I had no anticipation of what the results would be. Considerable care, based on six months' prior experience, was taken to see that the questions asked of informants were ones they could answer accurately. The only data included here which is based on questions the informants could not answer accurately concern age and the precise number of years ago that any event occurred. It does not seem likely that such errors are particularly relevant to the trends which are reported and analyzed here. Cross checks were made to determine that answers given by informants were truthful and almost always they were found to be so. However, a half-dozen cases were eliminated because of doubt about the truth of information given or because of internal contradictions in the answers given.

Figures on marriage forms among Santal in the traditional setting, i.e., Santal living in villages and practicing agriculture at least until the time they married, are based on a sample of fifty Santal.* All of these lived in villages at least twenty-five

---

* Of this sample of fifty, thirty-one became industrial workers after marriage and nineteen remained agriculturalists. The thirty-one were interviewed in *bustees*, town *bustees*, and Jamshedpur. The fifty interviewed were not selected by a format random sampling method. We simply went house-to-house at various times and questioned anyone who was home; no one refused to give us the

miles away from Jamshedpur, the nearest major city. The following frequences of the different forms of marriage were obtained from this sample:

DB	SB	TD	NB	Total Number
5 (10%)	20 (40%)	9 (18%)	16 (32%)	50 (100%)

Since the four varieties of marriage are graded in terms of cost, it is reasonable to plot farmer's per capita income against marriage form chosen to determine the degree to which income is associated with the form chosen. The figures given in Table 2 are in terms of maunds of husked paddy per person per year after taxation. A maund weighs approximately eighty lbs.

Converting these figures into percentages, one notes that eighty per cent of *DB* fall in the greater-than-thirty-maund category, eighty per cent of *SB* in the greater-than-ten-maund category, 55 per cent of *TD* in the greater-than-ten-maund category, and only twelve per cent of *NB* in the greater-than-ten-maund category. The association between marriage form and per capita income is obvious and consistent throughout. It suggests that per capita income is the largest single determinant of marriage-type choice.

Of the other possible countable determinants, the possibility that having either a father or a mother alive at the time of marriage might be significant was considered, since there were

---

information we requested. The same sampling procedure was used in the case of the *bustee* residents living in the *bustee* at the time of marriage. The nineteen were obtained from two villages in Mayurbhanj; fifteen of these were from Fanderkuta and the other four from the control village. In Fanderkuta the sample seemed ideal since data was obtained from every male in one "Section" (*tola* as in Hindi) of the village. However, over half of these informants had ultimately to be excluded from the sample since they had worked in surrounding mines prior to marriage.

TABLE 2

CHOICE OF MARRIAGE FORM BY FARMERS
BY PER CAPITA INCOME

Maunds per capita	Marriage Forms				Income Class Total
	DB	SB	TD	NB	
0–10	0	4	4	10	18
11–20	0	11	3	3	17
21–30	1	5	1	2	9
31–40	2	0	1	0	3
41	2	0	0	1	3
Total Number of Marriages	5	20	9	16	50

a few cases of comparatively well-off Santal without parents who had had an *NB*, and who explained that there was no one to arrange a marriage for them. Among the fifty sampled there were only six whose parents were both dead at the time of marriage. There were only three cases in which the father was living at the time of marriage and the mother not, and there were twenty-one cases in which only the mother was alive; however, there were no significant differences in these cases. It was therefore concluded that having a parent alive is seldom a determinant of marriage-type choice and that it is not generally relevant which parent is alive.[4]

One other type of countable information had to be considered: whether there was a shift in frequency during the forty-four-year period 1913 to 1957 in which these marriages occurred. The assembled data indicate that there were no sig-

---

[4] It might be significant in the very expensive *DB* but my sample was too small to detect its relevance.

nificant shifts in frequency during this period, nor were there any appreciable changes in the distribution of per capita income.

Before considering comparable data from the *bustee*, it is necessary to examine other partial determinants of marriage-type choice so that a controlled comparison can be made. The most significant of these secondary determinants derives from the expectation by the Santal community that members of high standing will validate their status by arranging high forms of marriage—*DB* or *SB*—for their children. These marriages are the occasion for great "pleasure" and the villagers would feel deprived if their "big people" (*maran hor*) were to deny them this opportunity. Since inherited office confers prestige and is partially independent of wealth, it may be presumed, though adequate statistical evidence is lacking, that the holders of hereditary office often feel compelled to choose more expensive forms than income alone would dictate. In support of this contention is the observation that of the seven *DB* of which I have knowledge, all involved the marriage of a son of a hereditary village officer and one was the son of a headman. Although shared values and understandings are prominent determinants of marriage type, idiosyncratic differences such as the desire for prestige may occasionally prove decisive. "Accidents" of contact and personality may compel a young couple to enter into a "love marriage" (*NB*) against parental wishes. Finally, there is the Santal belief that the higher the form of marriage, the greater its chances of lasting. It is possible, therefore, that differences in desire for marriage stability are a factor in marriage form chosen.

From the *bustees* a sample of forty-seven was obtained, with the majority from Daredih and the rest from nearby *bustees*. All were industrial workers living in a *bustee* at the time of marriage. They were selected by going house-to-house at various times and again no one refused to give us information. About 60 per cent of those Santal who come to Jamshedpur for industrial employment are unmarried when they arrive. The following frequencies of the different forms of marriage were obtained from this sample.

TABLE 3

CHOICE OF MARRIAGE FORM BY *BUSTEE* WORKERS

				Total Number	*Total Percentages*
DB	*SB*	*TD*	*NB*		
0 (0%)	6 (13%)	7 (15%)	34 (72%)	47	(100%)

RURAL FARM WORKERS

5 (10%)	20 (40%)	9 (18%)	16 (32%)	50	(100%)

A comparison of this data with that obtained from the village-farmer Santal shows a marked decrease in the more expensive and prestigeful *DB* and *SB* and a great increase in the cheapest and least prestigeful *NB* form, among *bustee* workers; this difference may also be regarded as a shift from arranged to unarranged marriages. If a Santal is going to have an arranged marriage of any grade, his parents or guardians must arrange it for him. The question therefore arises whether the shift to *NB* is primarily a choice made by parents or by the industrial workers who are their children. A number of lines of evidence, including the comments of workers, suggest that it is primarily their own option. While most Santal workers maintain a joint interest with their rural relatives in the family property and regularly send home some money and receive some rice, those workers who had arranged marriages sent home at that time a larger portion of their income than their fellows. Part of the money sent home was expended in the celebration of arranged marriages, which for immigrant workers almost always take place in their native villages. The relatively large amount of money sent home by those who had arranged marriages reflects exceptionally strong ties with the native village; however, even most of these workers have subsequently reduced their rural contribution as their own nuclear-family requirements increased.

The crucial fact indicated by the following table is that if one adds the industrial income of the workers at the time of their marriage to the farm income of their rural families, the combined per capita income is higher than that of the sample farmers. Since they must maintain separate households, these figures somewhat overstate available income for the workers. They clearly indicate, however, that the shift to NB cannot be attributed in any appreciable degree to lower income. Indeed even if one were to calculate per capita income of the *bustee* workers and their farming families solely on the rural income, the shift to NB could still not be accounted for simply by income.

Since those few migrant industrial workers who did have arranged marriages in fact sent home a large portion of their income before marrying, the inclusion of these resources in comparing marriage types seems realistic. Whereas farmers with per capita incomes of over ten maunds have only about 37% NB, 82% of the workers with similar income enter into such marriages. This comparison gives some indication of the degree to which the shift to NB runs counter to available income.

What must be explained is the shift away from the more

TABLE 4

COMPARISON OF PER CAPITA INCOME OF
BUSTEE WORKERS AND THEIR FARMING FAMILIES
WITH THAT OF PREVIOUS FARMER SAMPLE

(Income Categories in Maunds Per Capita) *

	0–10	11–20	20	Total
Farmers	36	34	30	100%
Workers	21	34	45	100%

expensive and prestigeful arranged forms of marriage, especially the SB form, to the cheaper, less prestigeful unarranged
NB in spite of increased per capita income. Furthermore, the
evidence indicates that the primary cause cannot be new values
gradually applied after taking up new employment. The key
factors responsible are spatial separation from parents or guardians and an independent income. Although the *bustee* Santal
maintains his connections with family in the native village
and seldom requests a division of the land, his independent
income provides him with the *de facto* opportunity to spend
as he pleases. Physical distance from his kin frees him from
their social control and the supporting authority of the villagers.
The shift to *NB* by the *bustee* Santal may then be viewed
partially as a decision not to share the major part of their income with their rural extended families. In the village they
would not have the financial independence to make such a
choice, nor would the social relations with kin and villagers
permit such a choice even with a separate income if they continued to live in the village. This interpretation is corroborated

* Industrial cash income was converted into husked paddy according to the
prevailing price of rice at the time of marriage and added to farm income in
husked rice after taxation.

by data on marriage obtained from those factory workers for whom the bustee is the native village. Of five such individuals, all had arranged *SB* marriages and had poured the major share of their income prior to marriage into the family coffers. Hence, it takes migration plus the separate income derived from industrial employment to produce a shift to love marriage.

Given that the conditions of migration to industrial employment provide an opportunity for the prospective groom to choose what form of marriage he desires, the question of why he tends to choose the unarranged *NB* remains. The answer appears to be that migration to industrial employment makes marriage primarily a matter of individual concern. In a variety of ways it weakens bonds with extended family, local lineage, and village. Since the bride will not live in the household or the village of the groom's parents, i.e., his native village, neither the parents nor the villagers are so concerned with her. Furthermore, residence in the *bustee* which, as we shall see, is not so solidary as a village, does not facilitate the reciprocal visiting between kin and fellow villagers of the couple which would normally follow a marriage tie. Since migration to industrial employment weakens traditional bonds of solidarity, it not only gives the prospective groom an opportunity to choose an unarranged marriage; it also makes groom, bride, kinsmen, and fellow villagers less desirous of an arranged marriage. All those social ties which are so dramatically expressed in marriage ceremonies and which are consistent with arranged marriages are virtually inoperative for migrants to the *bustee*. Unarranged marriages thus considered are a result of decreased solidarity resulting from migration to industrial employment.

Other considerations may be partially responsible for the

shift to *NB*. The Santal themselves point to the urgency felt by a new arrival in the *bustee* to get someone to cook and take care of the house; but the fact that the mean length of time immigrants spend in the *bustee* before marrying is 3.9 years and that only three of forty-seven are married within their first year of residence militates against this explanation. Any urgency that exists must be limited to the few immigrants who do not join the household of a married relative or friend, usually on a rent paying basis.

More important, freedom from parental and village restraint permits Santal men and women to meet each other and form liaisons. While this intermixing occurs to some extent even in traditional villages at festival and market time, women from moderately prosperous families have some difficulty escaping the watchful eyes of parents and kin. On the other hand, in the *bustee* no one is much interested in preventing liaisons, particularly if parents are not present. The resultant freedom is thus another manifestation of weakened ties with the traditional structure, ties which are not replaced by the *bustee*. Eighteen of the thirty-four *NB* marriages of the *bustee* Santal were contracted with working girls; it is probable that a large proportion of the remaining sixteen were with girls who were living in *bustees* while searching for work.

Evidence of one significant change emerged as an unanticipated consequence of the counting procedures used: between eleven and twenty-one years ago, about 64 per cent of the marriages in the *bustee* were *NB*, while in the period zero to ten years ago, 81 per cent were *NB*. Since per capita income was about the same during both these periods, it is possible that norms regarding marriage are gradually changing in the *bustee*.

What began as a shift resulting from migration to industrial employment and consequent weakening of traditional social bonds may have affected the norms by lessening the stigma of low status traditionally associated with the *NB*.

If one may use the term "modernization" to designate those indigenous developments or borrowings which are patently adaptive or characteristic of industrial urban societies, the shift to unarranged marriages with attenuated ceremonial is an example of modernization. Thus, while industrial development and migration to industrial employment have in a number of ways weakened Santal solidarity, the modernization which it has encouraged has in some respects suggested cultural alternatives not characteristic of traditional Hindu society. Insofar as this has been true, modernization has contributed to the maintenance of distinctiveness and solidarity and thereby inhibited assimilation. Many aspects of modernization, however, are likely to be equally operative among Hindu and Santal, especially in the long run, so that the cultures are made more alike.*

The Decline of Ceremonies in Bustee *and City*

Even a casual observer might note that ceremonies in the *bustee* as compared with those in the village are less well attended and often attenuated. As for the city Santal, they practice no communal forms of worship like those traditionally performed at the "Sacred Grove" as long as they remain in the city; often they do not even perform ancestor worship in

---

* Dr. Milton Singer called my attention to the significance of modernization with respect to my data on marriage and ceremonial and pointed out its significance in terms of acculturation and assimilation, though I am of course responsible for the form that his remarks have assumed above.

their Company houses. The temptation to interpret these changes as manifestations of increased secularity on a folk-urban continuum is great. However, a close look at the data suggests that the decline of ceremonies is not so much a question of increased secularity as it is a question of situational factors involved in migration to industrial employment. These factors operate directly to inhibit ceremonial practice and participation and operate indirectly to the same end by contributing to lack of solidarity in the *bustee* and city. Since ceremony both reflects and reinforces solidarity, its decline is both a cause and an effect of declining solidarity.

In the course of field work, I observed and participated in a number of ceremonies in the village, Fanderkuta, and the *bustee,* Daredih. Information concerning ceremonial practices was also obtained by interviews with informants from a variety of villages and *bustees.* Because of a suspicion that my presence, particularly in Daredih, had significantly altered the usual practice, my field assistant observed and reported on one ceremony, *Baha,* after I had left India. His report indicates that my suspicions were well founded. The reasons for decreased participation in and attenuation of ceremonies in the *bustee* as compared with the village are readily apparent if one examines the *Baha* ceremony as practiced in the two communities. Similar reports could be given of any of the other communal ceremonies.

Baha is the great spring festival celebrated in March* and ranking second in importance among annual ceremonies.† The word *Baha* means flower and refers here to the flowers of the Sal tree (*sarjom; shorea robusta*) and of the tree known as

---

* Actually in the Hindu month of *Phalgun* (February–March).

† The most important is known as *Sohrae* and will be briefly discussed later.

Matkom (Hindi: *Mahua*; *Bassia latifolia*) which are collected and distributed as part of the ceremony.**

The manifest purpose of the *Baha* ceremony is to request the deities (*bonga*) to prevent the occurrence of disease, a request which is made at every Santal ceremony and to provide good crops. The rites performed seem to express a general concern for the bounty of nature, respect for the village founder and his descendants, e.g., the headman and priest, and a reaffirmation of the ties of kinship, including an obligatory expression of joking behavior between "joking relatives" (*gonok' hor*). The respect shown for the village founder and his descendants may, of course, be regarded as reflecting and reinforcing village solidarity.

The festival as practiced in the village lasts two days. On the first day the priest (*Naeke*) bathes to purify himself and immerses for ritual purity the implements to be used in the rites. Most of the men gather at his house and five among them become "possessed" (*rum*). Each is possessed by one of the five major deities worshipped during *Baha*. One speaks and acts as Jaherera, the Goddess of the Sacred Grove; one as *Mōreko*, the Five; one as *Lita*; one as *Maran Buru*, Great Mountain; one as *Goram Bonga*, Old Deity, who is the spirit of Mạnjhi Hạram, the village founder. In the possessed state the five mediums go to the Sacred Grove to see that acts of purification previously performed there by the priest, including washing the three stones representing the deities of the grove and plastering the ground with purifying cow dung, have been properly performed.

On the next day the priest, accompanied by the same five

** The former is used for wood in building and for fuel and the leaves for making plates; the latter is the source of an intoxicating drink known as *Parua*.

men who are again possessed and amidst almost the entire village separated into lines of male and female dancers, proceeds to the Sacred Grove. The Goddess of the Sacred Grove carries a large wicker basket (*daurạ*) perhaps as a sign of the good harvest to come. The Five bring a bow and arrow signifying bountiful game, though hunting has ceased to be of economic significance.* *Liṭạ* brings an axe, the instrument which the Santal associate most closely with the clearing of new land. *Maraṅ Buru*, the national deity of the Santal, and *Goram Boṅga*, the godly embodiment of the village founder, carry sticks, perhaps as signs of their power. The five deities dance around the three stones which lie within a small shed open on all sides. The priest then sprinkles water on the stones and smears each with vermilion. He then "greets" (*johar*) each of the deities. The Five shoot an arrow at a Sal tree and the other deities rush up and smell the arrow to determine omens (*sagun*), which indicate whether the flowers of the tree would make a satisfactory offering. The deities then present flowers to the priest, who places them around the three stones. He makes three circles with rice flour around the stones and within each circle (*khond*) sun-dried rice and vermilion are applied. A large chicken is then brought to one of the circles and made to eat some of the sun-dried rice; then its head is cut off by the priest. As the blood drips into the circle the priest says, "Greeting *Maraṅ Buru*, in the name of *Baha* I am offering to you so that headache and stomach ache may not come to us; we give you that we may remain in good health." The same rite is repeated with the other two stones but the names of the

---

* Perhaps "The Five" have some connection with "The Five People" (*Mōre Hoṛ*) which, as explained, refers to the village council.

deities are not mentioned. After these rites the deities in the person of the five possessed ones eat the sun-dried rice that has been offered.

The priest then repairs to some open ground within the Sacred Grove which has been previously purified as described earlier; here he marks out with rice flour ten connected squares, in each of which he offers repeatedly to the five deities small or baby chickens donated by each family in the village. In prayer each of the deities is greeted and told that the offering is in the name of sowing. The priest says, "So many offerings are being made, are you not pleased?" The deities represented by the five possessed men then consume some of the sun-dried rice and the rest of the village men eat the remainder; the bodies of the chickens are also eaten by the villagers and the heads by the priest.

The final offering of the ceremony is conducted on the same day and in a similar manner but the offering is to the "boundary deities" (*sima bonga*). The names of the surrounding villages belonging to the same Pargana are mentioned in the offering as the priest exclaims, "Whatever deities you may be, let no illness or smallpox come to us."

The priest then tenders his respect to the spirit of the founder of the village, "Old Man Headman," by moving three times about the permanent shed (*manjhithan*) in which he dwells. The women then return to the Sacred Grove and receive flowers from the priest, who presents them with a greeting of respect like that made to an elder or a deity. Then, as the Santal say, "to show their respect for the priest," they all dance about him as he proceeds down the path of his section of the village; as he proceeds each woman washes his feet. The

77

practical jokes performed on each other by joking relatives such as pouring water down one another's back terminate the priest's procession.

After these rites the males of each household offer rice beer to their patrilineal ancestors. With religious obligations completed, dancing, singing, mutual visiting, eating, and drinking prevail and may continue through the evening and morning, to the exhaustion of the anthropologist but apparently not of the Santal participants.*

In the *bustee* celebration of *Baha*, the rites involving the five possessed men are eliminated; otherwise the rites performed are similar, the major difference being in the scale of participation. Since the rites of possession are eliminated, there is no occasion on the first day of the ceremony for all the villagers to gather at the priest's house; indeed, there are no rites to be performed on this day, so that the ceremony is condensed from two days to one. On the second day there is no great procession of dancing men and women accompanying the priest to the Sacred Grove; instead a few men and boys with no fanfare walk beside him to the grove. Those who go are almost all close patrilineal relatives of the priest for whom Daredih is a native village. Of the two non-relatives whom I observed accompanying the priest, one was the only immigrant worker who had bought farming land in Daredih; the other was one of the earliest immigrants who had for that reason become assistant headman (*jogmañjhi*) of the section (*tola*) of the *bustee* in which the immigrant workers live. Perhaps about half of the adult males of Daredih intermittently came and left during the performance of the rites. At this time one of the

---

* The rites reported here vary in minor detail from village to village but not in such a manner as to alter the comparison which is made here.

priest's brothers remarked that "the working people come only when it is time to eat." The priest also complained of this, as he had done at several other ceremonies. However, there were many more present than is usual, for my camera and the prospect of having a photograph taken which might later be obtained from me was a potent lure to these people. My assistant reported almost no workers present at these same rites after I had left India. The remainder of the ceremonies are performed as in the village, except that there is no procession of dancing men and women to lead the priest back into the village.

The attenuation of the ceremony and the relative non-participation of migrant industrial workers is not significantly the result of secularization. In spite of many interviews and casual discussions about the supernatural I found little evidence of decreased belief in the deities or the efficacy of rites. Also, many of these men occasionally returned to their villages for various festivals, and when I saw such men in their native villages I found their participation as ardent and regular as that of any villager.

In my view the most important cause of this attenuation of, and non-participation in, ceremonies is limited identification with the *bustee*, and there is evidence that this is the result of migration to industrial employment. The second most important cause of attenuation and non-participation is the time demands of industrial employment.

Those who participate most regularly and fully have strong grounds for identifying with the *bustee*. Almost all are natives of Daredih. The two other regular and full participants include the only immigrant worker who has bought land in Daredih and a very early immigrant who has become assistant headman.

The former, who had no land in his native village, frequently told me that for him Daredih was his village; the latter, by virtue of his position, of which he is extremely proud, is required to attend rites, and no doubt his status makes the *bustee* and its deities more his own than would otherwise be the case. The others, who have neither agricultural land nor position in Daredih, feel that it is not their village, that the local gods are not quite their gods, that the priest is not quite their priest, and that the founder of the village is not the founder of their village. This lack of commitment is reflected in both the attenuation of and non-participation in the various ceremonies of *Baha*. The Santal themselves say, "Here all are workers so we don't worship so much," or simply, "Here we don't worship so much."

This interpretation rather than secularization is supported by the observation that ancestor worship is generally practiced even by those who do not attend the community rites performed by the priest; in ancestor worship it is, of course, one's own ancestors who receive the offering. The failure to dance before the priest's house and the failure to provide him with a dancing procession to and from the Sacred Grove are indications that he is not quite their priest; the same explanation accounts for their frequent failure to contribute to the sacrifices on behalf of the *bustee*. Indeed, the Santal themselves regard all of these acts as signs of respect to the village leaders, and as already indicated, the priest often complains on this score.

Nor can all these acts, which both express and serve to weaken the solidarity of Daredih, be entirely due to the time demands of industrial employment. The priest is himself an industrial worker, as are many of his patrilineal relatives who live in Daredih, and they are regular participants. Also, the number of immigrant workers present when it comes time to eat the offerings that have been made, drink the rice beer which has been offered, and join in secular dancing for pleasure is invariably greater than those present during the performance of village ceremonials.

It is not that the immigrant workers regard it as wrong to worship the deities of the *bustee*'s Sacred Grove or to offer respect to its priest and founder; on occasion and in varying degrees they will do both. Except for "Old Man Headman" and the boundary deities, the same beings are celebrated in their native villages. It is rather a question of having less attachment than of opposition. As these workers say when asked about non-participation, "It is all right because all is being done properly in my native village."

Typically, migration to industrial employment does not result in acquisition of agricultural land at the new place of residence; both limited availability of land in such areas as well as alternative employment make this difficult. Lack of agricultural land belonging to the *bustee* limits identification. Ownership of such land has the opposite effect; as the regular attendance at Daredih's communal ceremonies by immigrant workers who had purchased land there tends to show. Similarly, the Santal have a long history of migration, and Santal who move to a new village where they acquire land show none of the signs of lack of identification characteristic of immigrant workers in Daredih. Thus it is not simply migration which is responsible for diminished solidarity, but migration to industrial employment.

The *Baha* festival was, of course, not the only ceremonial casualty of migration to industrial employment of which I saw evidence at Daredih. At the great *Sohrae* festival, held in October when the harvest is in, the final fourth day's rites are eliminated; these are primarily concerned with collecting and stealing rice beer and food from all the houses. During this festival a rite is performed in which the villagers' cows are made to walk over an area where some eggs have been placed. The owner of the cow which first breaks an egg is considered propitious, and he is required to repay the deities for his good fortune by providing the rice beer to be offered on the following year. At the ceremony in Daredih few were in attendance, and that few did not include the immigrant worker whose cow had previously broken the egg, so that another man had to provide the rice beer. Finally, there was a noisy dispute within the *bustee* because the immigrant workers assembled for dancing on the dancing ground (*akhra*) in their section rather than before the house of the headman, as they should have done according to tradition.

At the festival of Sakrat in mid-February, the third most elaborate ceremony, the custom of going house-to-house to collect rice beer is shortened from three days to one day; in addition, a rite in which arrows are shot at pole targets is not practiced. At a village not half a mile further away from the town and only a short distance from Daredih arrow-shooting is practiced; but in this village almost all are native villagers practicing agriculture though the headman and a few others are factory workers besides being farmers. This negative instance of attenuation and non-participation provides further proof of the critical significance of migration to industrial employment.

If limited identification with the *bustee* is primarily responsible for the decline of ceremony, the time demands of industrial employment have been an unwitting accomplice. The time demands of factory employment are in certain critical ways different than those of agricultural labor. For example, TISCO works on three eight-hour shifts, while the hours of agricultural labor are typically identical for all. Furthermore, in a number of departments of a steel mill there are no occasions, barring a strike, when all work comes to a standstill. This industrial situation makes it impossible for all Santal workers of the community to be present for a ceremony during any fixed period. Some departments give a leave of absence to all their workers for major Hindu festivals, but Santal ceremonials do not always coincide in time with Hindu ones. Nor could such an adjustment, if desired, be easily made, since Santal villages have no fixed days for their ceremonies and each village chooses a day or several days within the appointed month during which the villagers will be free of agricultural labor.

There is a third factor to be taken account of, though it is so entwined with lack of identification that it may only be distinguished analytically. Since the immigrant workers seldom have agricultural land in the *bustee*, some of the rites performed at various ceremonies which concern agricultural abundance, such as *Baha*, are of diminished interest. To be sure, they probably have land in their native village contributing to their own and their relatives' income, but, as they remark, "It is all right not to participate here because it is all being done properly in my native village." This attitude is closely related to lack of identification since, as already indicated, the place where one has land is likely to be regarded as one's own village. Connected with this attitude is the immigrant worker's intention of eventually retiring to his native village to live off the land. He may even look forward to purchasing his land with his industrial earnings.

83

There are a few observations concerning ceremonial practice which apply to all the city Santal (excluding, of course, those who live in town *bustees*). We have seen that the city Santal are not even a community to the degree that the *bustee* Santal are; they do not, for the most part, live side-by-side, they have no headman or priest and they have no Sacred Grove in which to assemble for community worship. The practice of community worship is ruled out for lack of physical facilities, but as we have seen from our examination of the *bustee*, there is little reason to think that their presence would be sufficient to maintain ceremonial practice and participation at the level obtained in rural villages.

What is most striking about the city Santal is that they do not practice ancestor worship in their Company houses. Their explanation of this, with a little elaboration, appears to me to be an adequate one. They say, "Who knows whose houses these were before we got here—they are not our houses. That is why we do not worship here." It will be recalled that ancestor worship is performed behind a wall dividing off a portion of the main room of the house and known as "inside" (*bhitạr*; Santali and Hindi = "inside"). The same word is used to refer to secret rites and deities of a family and of a local lineage, i.e., when a question touches on such things they will say you are asking an "inside" question. It will also be recalled that this "inside" portion of the house must be guarded against pollution by menstruating women. Since it is not permissible to erect such a wall within a company house, again physical facilities in the city render traditional practice difficult. But more than the particular difficulty of lack of a wall, there is a general question of pollution. Not only does the company house not provide a proper sanctuary for the "inside" rites of the local lineage, but it is filled with the pollution of some unknown *Diku* caste.

Another obstacle to worship that the city Santal encounter is that it is illegal to brew rice beer in the city. This restriction is also cited by the city Santal as a reason why they do not practice ancestor worship. On several occasions the police have interfered with its manufacture in town *bustees*.

Were the city Santal able to live side by side in a single section of the city and to build their own houses, they might at least attain the solidarity of the *bustee* communities. But the policy of alloting houses follows the universalistic principles which TISCO has deliberately fostered. Houses are assigned according to rank in the factory hierarchy and seniority, with personal preference a minor consideration. Thus, the Santal and other ethnic groups are generally dispersed. Under these circumstances it is not surprising that most of those Santal who have chosen to live in Company houses are relatively well educated and highly acculturated; nor is it surprising that the lack of a Santal community in the city is contributing markedly to the Hinduization of the Santal children living there.

Migration to industrial employment has acted as a sociocultural solvent significantly affecting marriage and ceremonial patterns. Weber's notion of its importance is borne out, but in the cases examined it does not appear to be "the mere fact of living in quite different surroundings" which accounts for its significance. Here its effect seems largely due to its tendency to disrupt traditional social bonds. In the absence of such disruption, as in the case of the natives of Daredih, it seems that traditional practices evolved in a context far removed from urban-industrial conditions are surprisingly viable. These findings support Nash's contentions about the importance of migration in producing change and, conversely, provide additional evidence of how little change may accompany industrial employment in the absence of migration. Since rural migration produces none of the effects of migration to industrial employment and since industrial employment per se does not produce the changes described either, the combination must be studied in its own right.

Chapter 5 The Extent of Hindu Absorption

The effects of migration to industrial employment thus far analyzed have been to accelerate the decline of Santal solidarity among the Santal generally and especially among Santal industrial workers. It has thus furthered the same tendency which the closure of the political rank path and the spread of the market and of increased wealth differences accelerated. Before moving on, it is useful to consider how much Hindu social absorption has accompanied this decline in solidarity.

Indian census material on religious identification is often cited as evidence of Hindu social absorption. Converting such figures on the southern Santal to percentages, the following table can be constructed. Conclusions from these figures, which indicate very little in the way of a trend, must be drawn with extreme caution.

My own field observations suggest that these figures do not reflect major changes in religious belief and practice. There are virtually no villages where half or even one-tenth of the Santal practice Hindu rituals distinct from the ritual practices of the other Santal residents, nor is there some sizable propor-

TABLE 5

PERCENTAGE OF SANTAL RETURNED AS HINDU

(Census of India 1931)*

	1901	1911	1921	1931
Orissa	44	46	43	48
Chota Nagpur Feudatory States				
(Seraikela, Kharswan)		0	18	48
Singhbhum	16	3	56	23

tion of villages which follow distinctively Hindu religious practices. I have heard of only one Santal village within the territory occupied by the southern Santal which has abandoned traditional forms of worship and become thoroughly Hinduized. In 1916 Roy reported the conversion to Hinduism of a number of Santal in a Hindu village in Orissa; they were served by an outcast Brahman priest.[1] I met only one Santal who had taken up Hindu religious practices, and he lived in the city of Jamshedpur. Nowhere that I went were Santal served by Brahmans, though in some areas Santal families are occasionally visited by members of the Potkar caste, who bring messages from the dead for a fee. The Santal also employ females of various low Hindu castes to deliver their children and sometimes patronize Hindu practitioners of traditional medicine (*Kubraj*; Hindi).

It is true that until recently the Santal in large numbers took part, in their own way, in various Hindu festivals. At many of the major Hindu festivals the Santal would assemble for mixed dancing, and some would become possessed and speak

---

* More recent census figures do not contain this information because "caste has been abolished" as a legal entity.

[1] Roy, 1916.

in the name of the Hindu deities invoked. Although this activity has recently been somewhat curtailed for reasons soon to be discussed, it is still possible to observe Santal worshipping Jugganath at the Cart Festival (*Rath Jatra*) in Baripoda, the capital of Mayurbhanj. Many Santal, even in villages where there are few Hindus, may also be seen immersing the Hindu Tusu goddess. In spite of these activities, in which most Santal have engaged, and even though all Santal ceremonies have some Hindu elements, almost all southern Santal have remained firmly attached to their own deities, and there have been no mass conversions.

The Indian government's figures on Hindu religious identification are largely an artifice of census methods, and since at least the 1920's, often of coercion as well. Culshaw, for example, commments that:

> The prevailing Indian identification of race with religion has caused some confusion in their [the Santals'] minds, but the fact that about 50 per cent of Santal were returned in 1931 as Hindus and most of the remainder as followers of tribal religion indicated the heightened political consciousness of the enumerators more than any real division within the tribe.[2]

Many Santal reported to me that they were pressured by local Hindu authorities to register themselves as Hindus. Others claimed that ignorance played a major role in the returns; the census-takers asked, "What is your religion?" (*Dhorom*; Oriya), and most Santal, it is said, did not understand this word. When it was explained they would reply "Santal religion," and the census-taker would then say, "That is your caste (*jāti*), not

[2] Culshaw 1949:15.

your religion. Are you Hindu, Muslim, Christian, or what?" By this means the census-takers might obtain the desired result. However, it should be remembered that neither Culshaw, who is a Christian missionary, nor the presently very communally oriented Santal are disinterested observers.

There is no question that since the 1920's at least, Hindu organizations like Arya Samaj have actively campaigned to get tribals to declare themselves as Hindus. Such declarations were regarded as demonstrations of national unity and as refutations of the charge that India was so culturally and socially diverse as to be incapable of nationhood. In view of Hindu pressures and census irregularities, the returns reported may at the most indicate that Santals were finding it increasingly difficult to muster the solidarity to resist Hindu pressure for common religious identification. At the very least, the returns may simply reflect Hindu pressure generated by the Independence Movement.

In spite of the manifold pressures operating to weaken Santal solidarity, there are few cases of actual social absorption. Apparently, the endogenous forces contributing to solidarity have been sufficient to prevent this from happening. However, in view of the experience of other tribes and because of the increase in centrifugal pressures created by industrial employment, it appears that further social absorption was imminent. Certainly centrifugal pressures had increased, and if the political rank path had not suddenly reopened in the 1930's, it seems likely that the Santal would have become as Hinduized as their neighbors, the Bhumij.

3

the new solidarity

Chapter 6 The Political Rank Path

In the 1930's, political events external to Santal society began to alter profoundly the path that the Santal were treading. What one observes today instead of acculturation and assimilation is a native sociocultural resurgence, but one filled with apparently paradoxical elements. Though I was unaware of it at the time, the first Santal I met in Jamshedpur confronted me in the course of a few weeks with all of the fundamental questions which this resurgence poses. To introduce these questions I will recount this experience, and with the benefit of hindsight, suggest the directions which answers to the questions posed will take.

It was October of 1957 when I arrived at Jamshedpur, and the city was preparing for Durga Puja, the most elaborately celebrated Hindu festival in Jamshedpur. Company officials had thoughtfully provided me with my first Santal informant, clearly a good model of Company efforts in behalf of tribals. Mr. F. came to Jamshedpur with a high-school education and received further training in the TISCO apprentice school. He had served for fifteen years in the brick kiln works and was then in line for promotion to assistant supervisor. His work record was excellent, including an award of Rs. 25 and special commendation for having suggested an improvement in the brick-making process. Fortunately for me, Mr. F. spoke adequate English in addition to excellent Hindi, Bengali, Oriya, and three Mundari languages—his own (Santal), Ho, and Mundari.

I was impressed with his intelligence and noticed that he seemed highly acculturated, though at that early stage of our relationship I could not point to specific Hindu practices which marked this acculturation; it was rather an impression based upon bearing and gesture. Later my impression of Mr. F.'s Hinduization was repeatedly confirmed. I learned that he had been sent to live with a Brahmin family as a small boy. I recall a discussion among Mr. F., five other Santal, and me in which the rites of Santal local lineages were discussed; Mr. F. alone insisted that the rites of some lineages, especially his own, were purer and higher than those of other lineages. The other Santal present argued in traditional Santal fashion that each thinks his own lineage best but that none is better than any other. The strongest confirmation of my impression is that it is shared by less acculturated Santal. One young man who had married a relative of Mr. F. refused to visit Mr. F., despite the urging of his wife, who had lived for some years in Mr. F.'s house and wished to visit. It was this young man who remarked that Mr. F. was so much like a *diku*, that "before him I feel like a black Santal."

But it was not Mr. F.'s acculturation which puzzled me. The literature on acculturation of Indian tribals is replete with such cases and we are not without some knowledge of the basis of this acculturation. It was rather the vehemence of his objection to Santal attendance and participation in the Durga Puja ceremonies which I could not account for. He told me that the celebration was a "lure and a trap for tribals." When I asked him if other Santal felt similarly he described the manner in which word against attendance and participation was being spread throughout the area by Santal and other tribal headmen and men of influence. Surprisingly, he and his family attended the ceremonies and so did a number of other Santal from the city and surrounding countryside, including workers from the *bustees*. The word, however, had been circulated among tribals that they should not attend and should under no conditions participate by performing group dances or becoming possessed, as was their custom. Some did refrain from attendance as urged, and no tribals performed group dances or became possessed.

Why should Mr. F., one of the most acculturated Santal, vehemently oppose tribal attendance and participation in the Hindu celebration? It seemed to me that the most acculturated would surely be most in favor of acculturation. I asked Mr. F. why he opposed attendance and participation. He said, "It is bad for Santal and other tribals to be present because they are mostly 'ignorant' people and on such occasions are taken advantage of by numerous Hindus who wheedle away their earnings." While this explanation justified his own attendance since he is not "ignorant," taken at face value it hardly seems to account for the organized opposition to tribal attendance and the particular emphasis against participation in the ceremonies. In addition Mr. F.'s fears that his fellow tribals would be gulled by the Hindus seemed inappropriate, since most of the tribals of the area who might attend were either workers in daily contact with Hindus or farmers who live near Jamshedpur, or villagers who run the risk of being swindled

95

weekly at various markets. Santal attendance at Durga Puja could hardly present Hindus with unprecedented opportunities to take advantage of tribals. Nevertheless, as I shall show later, a less literal interpretation of Mr. F.'s remarks accounts rather well, at least in part, for his opposition.

An event a few days after the Durga Puja provides some clues about Mr. F.'s opposition. He came to see me and to return a book on the Santal which he had borrowed. I asked what he thought of the book and he said, "It is very bad; it says that 'aboriginals' (*ādibāsī*; Hindi) only progress when in the presence of Hindus. For example, it says that we have borrowed 'vermilion' from the Hindus when we think it is they who have borrowed it from us." I asked him to show me those portions of the book to which he took exception, and he pointed to the section dealing with acculturation. He was somewhat mistaken in attributing to the author an attitude favoring acculturation; both his limited command of English and his knowledge of the predominant Hindu position regarding acculturation probably influenced his interpretation. Mr. F. was not willing to let the matter rest with the mere comment that the book was bad, and he caused me some alarm by proposing to read the portions of the book he opposed before the local branch of the tribal Jharkhand political party. His objective was to obtain a declaration of protest against the book to be forwarded to the Central Government. It is not now important that I managed to dissuade him from such action. But that a sophisticated Santal could contemplate such action suggests institutionalized opposition to acculturation. It further suggests a connection between this opposition and political objectives. It was only later that I learned that the Jharkhand party had spearheaded the drive to prevent tribal attendance and participation at the Durga Puja festival. One acculturated Santal opposing acculturation is a mystery which the anthropologist, with his concern for custom, might choose to ignore; but I met such acculturated Santal everywhere, and they proved the most militant opponents of acculturation; indeed, the least militant proved to be the least acculturated and most isolated villagers. The ordinary Santal, a little behind the times, were just geting on to emulation while the elite maneuvered a volte-face. Events of the 1930's explain this change.

With the approach of independence in the 1930's a new political rank path opened. The British Raj was gradually relinquishing power, and it became evident to sophisticated observers that the days of the princely rulers of Mayurbhanj, Seraikela, and Kharswan were numbered. The day of democratic election was dawning in India. In the north, with headquarters in Ranchi, the Oxford-educated and Christian Munda, Jai Pal Singh, organized an "aboriginal" political party. The proclaimed aim of the party was and is to establish a tribally dominated state within the Indian Union. Such a state would include the geographical area known as the Chotanagpur Plateau and roughly referred to in Indian literature as the Jharkhand. It would include much of southern Bihar, northern Orissa and a thin slice of the western portion of West Bengal. In such a state, which incidentally would contain Jamshedpur and some of the richest mineral deposits in India, tribal peoples would be in a near majority.

The "likenesses" shared by the Mundari-speaking peoples who comprise most of the tribal population of the Jharkhand were available as cultural cement. In the north, Jai Pal successfully brought together the Mundari-speaking Munda and Santal as well as the Dravidian-speaking Oraon, who had long lived

97

among the Munda and adopted many Mundari traits. In the south he was able to convince the leading members of the Santal and Ho elite to join his political movement. Numerous consultations and meetings were held, a party organization was established near Jamshedpur, and campaigns were planned for Singhbhum and Mayurbhanj. Not only were there political offices of considerable power to fill by democratic elections, but there were a number of special reserved seats for "aboriginals." The rise of Jai Pal and his Jharkhand party meant that the Santal had to make a choice between joining a Hindu-dominated party such as the Congress party or supporting an "aboriginal" party of their own. A substantial majority have continuously decided on the latter course.

The initiative to join politically with other tribals has come primarily from the elite. In a tribally-dominated state they envisage themselves as occupying the most powerful positions with unprecedented opportunity for personal and tribal rank improvement. Political democracy reawakened the old dreams of independence and power. While the leading emulators were the Santal traditional and newly educated elite, and the latter most conspicuously alienated from their fellows with respect to culture, neither could look upon the social encroachment of Hindu society with favor. They, above all, had a vested interest in traditional social positions of power and prestige and therefore most to lose from such encroachment. Furthermore, even had they wished to lead their people into a Hindu-dominated political movement, it is doubtful that they would have been able to bring along the mass of uneducated and relatively unacculturated Santal, particularly in competition with a specifically tribal political organization. The fear and hatred of the *diku* are not easily exorcised. A few elite Santal have sought to further their careers by bringing their fellows into the Congress party, but their success has been extremely limited and the personal price they have been made to pay has been enormous. Some of these need fear for their lives outside the confines of their own village.

Since its inception the Jharkhand party has succeeded in electing many candidates to the state legislatures of Bihar and Orissa. In Bihar, after the election of 1956 the Jharkhand party emerged as second only to the Congress in number of seats; in Orissa enough representatives were elected to make Jharkhand support necessary for any party in power to stay in power. A few members have been elected to the *Lok Sabha*, the Indian equivalent of the House of Commons. Though the Jharkhand party has improved its position in each election it failed during the course of the states' reorganization after independence to achieve a Jharkhand state. Nevertheless, this remains the ostensible aim of the party. In practice the party works for such special benefits for "aboriginals" as scholarships, increased opportunities in industry, wells and irrigation facilities, etc. In a small way there have been accomplishments, and no doubt the efforts of the Jharkhand party have made a difference; fortunately for (and perhaps as a concession to) the party, the official Congress position is also to "raise the level" of the aboriginals by precisely the means favored by the Jharkhand party. In fact, the most effective complaint of the Jharkhand against the Congress has been the latter's hostility to a Jharkhand state rather than opposition to specific tribal welfare measures.

Most of the elective offices have been filled by the educated elite. Coveted positions within the party are also largely held by such acculturated Santal, with the lower officials and unpaid volunteers drawn from all levels of the society. There are, therefore, abundant immediate rewards to be derived from the political movement in addition to the dreams of power and glory in an "aboriginal" state. Besides the economic and prestige awards stemming from political action there are newly discovered rewards which are derived from a cultural creativity closely connected with political objectives.

Jamshedpur and industrial employment have been shown to have increased both the incentive and the opportunity for education. In the absence of a political rank path, i.e., prior to the 1930's, the effect of this increase in education was seen to be essentially divisive and as accelerating already existing centrifugal tendencies. But now the educated Santal are those most capable of becoming leaders in the Jharkhand movement. Since Jamshedpur and its environs have relatively many educated Santal, it is one of the areas where Jharkhand activity is most intense. It is also, of course, an area where tribals are densely concentrated and thus an opportune point for political headquarters. A building to serve as the headquarters of the Jharkhand party within the southern portion of the Chotanagpur Plateau has been built just outside Jamshedpur, incidentally with financial aid from the astute TISCO officials, who also contribute substantially to the Congress. Major mass meetings which attract not only the bulk of the tribal working force, but also villagers from as far away as southern Mayurbhanj, are held near a Santal *bustee* just beyond Jamshedpur. One TISCO worker from a *bustee* has achieved the coveted position of Member of the Bihar Legislative Assembly (MLA). Many other *bustee* dwellers are active party workers, and the recent burst of cultural creativity is particularly vital around Jamshedpur.

Jamshedpur has further contributed to the new political movement and the new solidarity by the characteristics of its own rank path. The first of these characteristics, even prior to the present period, must have mitigated the centrifugal tendencies present and may even have affected the decision of the Santal elite to support the Jharkhand movement. I refer to the fact that rank in Jamshedpur is so largely dependent on wealth translated into appropriate material possessions, and so little dependent on the attributes of high Hinduism or even caste membership. One may at every turn observe the subservience of devout Brahmans to those of lower caste and even to "Harijans" who hold higher positions in the company hierarchy. Prior to the Jharkhand movement the observation of rank in Jamshedpur could only lessen the tendency toward emulating high Hinduism. The aspiring Santal who was well acquainted with Jamshedpur might adopt Western clothing, an automobile or motorcycle, and a *pukha* house (one with modern facilities) rather than vegetarianism, teetotalism, and a sacred thread; he might observe that the Parsees, Europeans, and Westernized Hindus did not pay a price in rank for the lack of high Hindu attributes. But in the context of a market economy and without a political rank path to draw the Santal and other tribals together, these observations suggest individual mobility rather than a socio-cultural movement aimed at improving the rank of tribals as a group; hence without a political rank path this characteristic did not of itself produce a new solidarity. Nevertheless it seems probable that the Jamshedpur experience made the maintenance of tribal solidarity appear consistent with the attainment of superior rank.

A second characteristic of Jamshedpur which has favored the Jharkhand movement and therefore tribal and Santal solidarity is the extreme importance of political power in determining the outcome of labor disputes. The Santal and other tribals were strong supporters of the Tata Workers Union as long as it remained politically unaffiliated. After independence it became a Congress union, and since Congress is the major opponent of the Jharkhand party, a threat to the Jharkhand movement. At the time of my field work the Jharkhand party began the formation of a "workers association" to counter this threat. There is considerable latent support for this development because most tribals are opposed to the present leadership of the Tata Workers Union, which they regard as inattentive to their needs and biased against them. They accuse various leaders of the union of giving special preference to members of their own caste or people from their own province. Whether due to Jharkhand efforts or not, a number of special considerations for "aboriginals" have improved the economic prospects for tribals in Jamshedpur. The state government has exerted pressure on TISCO and other firms to hire "aboriginals" and to provide evidence that they are being trained for and given jobs of high pay and status. To this end TISCO is made to furnish periodic reports indicating the number of "aboriginals" employed and their positions in the company hierarchy. With TISCO's help, local tribal leaders have established an "*Ādibāsī*" Cooperative Society, a savings and loan association to which many tribals have entrusted their savings. Thus, with the help of political organization, the special status of "aboriginals" has been made to confer special benefits—some of which might possibly have been forthcoming anyway, since the welfare state ideology is dominant in India, and is backed by official tradition of special benefits to "scheduled" tribes and castes. In any case, the general context within which the Jharkhand worked was at least to this extent favorable to the realization of its aims.

While the Santal industrial workers are substantially behind Jharkhand, the social schism between the elite and ordinary Santal, which is generally reflected as leaders and followers in the Jharkhand movement, is a source of disintegrative tendencies. Despite general support there are complaints that the leaders are only out to further their own ends. These sentiments are reinforced by a number of well-known cases in which leaders have pocketed funds collected for the party. There is also some tendency, particularly among the city Santal, to support third parties which are militantly pro-worker, especially when the local Jharkhand candidate has little chance of winning; this is most likely to be the case where "aboriginals" are in a minority, as in the city.

The schism between elite and non-elite is a continuing problem for the political movement, and the success which that movement has had in entering the promising new political rank path must have accentuated the ever-present conflict between emulation of the Hindus and tribal solidarity: while clearly calling for renewed solidarity to attain political success, the movement equally demanded emulation and abandonment of distinctive characteristics to validate the status which increased political power promised. This emulation-solidarity conflict was particularly serious among the Santal elite. About them were living examples indicating that emulation of Hindus led eventually to social absorption. Furthermore they were aware of the increasing cultural and consequent social schism between themselves and the common Santal. Rank improvement by passing into the Hindu fold still constituted an alluring prospect. Furthermore, Hindu values and attitudes had been

103

so deeply internalized that even had they lost their rank value the conflict with solidarity would have persisted. But rank improvement via political success required the maintenance and even the increase of solidarity and this in turn required checking and even reversing the tendency to emulate. Since the elite are themselves the greatest emulators and those who have most internalized Hindu values, and at the same time those who have the greatest stake in political success, it is among them that the emulation-solidarity conflict is most intense.

The cultural creativity which has accompanied the Jharkhand political movement has certain characteristics which may be regarded as attempts to resolve this conflict. It may also be that the psychological tension arising from this conflict is largely responsible for the dynamism and creativity which the movement has displayed. What has been accomplished culturally may properly be termed an emergent "great tradition."[1]

---

[1] Redfield and Singer 1954.

Chapter 7   The "Great Tradition"

One might say that the Santal have been in search of a "great tradition" since the time that they conceded the social and cultural superiority of their Hindu neighbors. Having taken much from these neighbors, but desirous of maintaining their identity, they decided to create a "great tradition" of their own rather than accept the one belonging to their neighbors. There is, for example, an attempt to codify Santal traditions in writing and even the development of a distinctive script in which to record these traditions. In place of an essentially inexplicit religious ideology expressed in ritual, there is the development of an explicit religious ideology with an emphasis on morality. There is also the elaboration of literary forms wholly unlike the unpretentious traditional ones. Paradoxically, while these developments involve rejection of numerous Hindu practices, they introduce fundamental beliefs and values of Hinduism which previously had made hardly any progress among the Santal. Thus, while distinctive traits are re-emphasized, the configurations and orientation of Santal culture become somewhat more like those of the Hindus. However, innovative patterns are also arising, particularly through the fusing of traditional and Hindu patterns.

I do not want to portray this striking cultural development as more profane than it is by giving undue emphasis to its connections with political objectives and pursuit of rank. Nevertheless, one must begin by recognizing that this is its source. As very grossly advocated by a somewhat naïve Santal industrial worker who has become a "Member of the Legislative Assembly," the movement is spoken of in the following terms: "We should not leave our religion; we should continue to use rice beer; we should have our worship at the Sacred Grove; also we should not stop eating beef. If we stop eating it our Santal caste will be gone. We will call our religion *Sarna Dhorom** and will tell everyone that our religion is *Sarna Dhorom*." Another Santal entered the conversation saying, "Yes, like Mussulman *Dhorom*, Christian *Dhorom*, so we will call ours *Sarna Dhorom*." A third Santal said, "Yes, if we say *Santal Dhorom*, that is our caste; as the Christians have a church, so our 'temple' (*mandir*; Hindi) is the Sacred Grove." The MLA brought the conversation to a close and down to "practical" matters by saying: "We will maintain our 'drama club'; we will keep our 'culture'; if we keep our 'culture' the government will give us money; if you do a drama I will bring big officers of the Jharkhand party to see."

There are sections of Jharkhand political rallies with such a concentration on culture that one might imagine himself at a festival rather than a political meeting. The local club may perform a play at such a meeting; traditional dances may be

---

* *Sarna* is the Munda word for "Sacred Grove" (*Jaher* in Santali); *Dhorom* is the Oriya form meaning roughly "religion."

arranged by Jharkhand leaders, some of whom would themselves be ashamed to dance. So potent a political weapon is
culture that the great crime of a Santal-elected official who went
over to the Congress was that he wrote a pamphlet in which
he argued that the Mundari languages were related to Oriya.

Though the cultural movement is intimately connected with
politics, the elite who are sparking the movement are quite
sincere in their cultural efforts; men are indeed usually capable
of sincerely believing in that which is necessary to the pursuit
of rank. The sophisticated Santal believes that he is contributing to a resurgence of tribal tradition and at the same time
raising it to a higher level. And so he is. But neither the
grounds on which he justifies his act nor its effect are the sufficient causes of the cultural movement. Yet despite the basically
political source of its energy, the cultural movement has acquired an impetus of its own. There is honor to be gained
through cultural creativity, and the Santal elite have begun to
experience the pleasure of cultural innovation per se.

The distinctive traits re-emphasized in the new movement
are chiefly those mentioned by the MLA whose remarks are
recorded above. They are beef eating and cow sacrifice, traditional dances, drinking and offering rice beer, and worship of
the traditional gods at the Sacred Grove. The low rank value
of these traits makes them ideal boundary markers. These traits
serve not only to bind together the Santal but are held in common with most of the tribes which support the Jharkhand
movement. They are the banners under which the Jharkhanders
march, and their contrast with Hindu banners is conspicuous.
Unfortunately, beef eating and dancing are particularly difficult
for the educated elite, so that their preaching is often better

than their practice. For them these are the unresolvable neces-
sities of the new rank path. Some of these Santal whom we
met in 1957 had just begun to eat beef again; happily, one
city Santal read in a magazine about the virtues of beef eating
for health, and his discovery quickly diffused among the rest
of the city Santal. Once I saw a young party activist who had
grown up during the Jharkhand movement persuading an older
Santal with a few years of education that he must take up
beef eating again if he wished to preserve the Santal caste. The
emphasis given to these distinctive traits serves, of course, not
only to keep Santal and Hindu apart but also to narrow the
gap between the elite and the ordinary Santal.

One of the fundamental changes being wrought in Santal
culture is an increased emphasis on work, study, and rank attainment and a concomitant discouragement of "pleasure." A
number of recent songs like the following carry this message.

At work time I become drunk and forget my work.
At the time for study I spent my time making friends;
I forgot all about reading and writing.

Babu, boys the same age as you have become pundits at Tata school.
Oh brother in the city of Delhi they have become members of parlia-
ment.
Oh brother you were born in a long village.
Oh brother you grew up among friends.
Oh brother you have only become a pundit in divorced women.

Notice in the following song carrying a message like those
above the use of un-Santal-like metaphors in the manner of
the new "great tradition."

You want to reach the fruit,
Without effort you can't reach the higher fruit.
Make your mind hard!
Release your soul!
Be energetic with your body!
Then you shall reach the fruit which hangs high.

Other songs with Calypso-like Santal manner carry the message of Jharkhand, the necessity of maintaining distinctiveness, the moral-religious connection, and in some cases the new great-traditional style. Notice in particular the intermingling of these themes in these stanzas:

We are natives of this country,
Yet they are driving us out;
They are driving us from our birthplace.
Be learned, brother, be knowing, be a man.

Jai Pal Singh protects us against other castes.
Raghnath Murmu [the founder of a cultural organization] will
make us learned and wise.

In the country of Dhalbhum the *Tamak* [a kind of drum] sounds.
In Hanuman's forest the Sakwa [a wild buffalo horn] sounds.
In the "aboriginal" land the deer are devouring the forest.
Sam and Supai [two Jharkhand candidates] sound the bell;
Come great Jai Pal and sound the *Sakwa* to drive the deer away.

For the man of today, *haeri haeri* [ai ai]
On a tree of trouble grows troubled fruit.
Because of sin the body is pained, *haeri haeri*.
Since we are poor we get only *matkom lathe* [a nearly inedible fruit
from which the liquor *parua* is made].

Millet we never get.
Day by day we starve and become desiccated, *haeri.*
Dirty grass huts, poverty, and sickness cause us to moan, *haeri.*
Continuous sickness follows us all our life.
Who will cure this?

Maran Buru is like an *ojha* [medicine man in Santali and Hindi]
He will end this sickness.
Let us drive out this evil by applying our intelligence.
Let us drive it out with our sacred prayers.
This religion will wipe away the sin.
With the help of religion let us bid this evil go.
Then we will obtain heaven's reward, god-given love and joy.
Through religion the poverty and sickness of hell will vanish.

This last song in particular is interspersed with Oriya and Sanskritic words. It also introduces heaven and hell, neither of which has a place in the traditional religion; but Maran Buru, the tribal deity of the Santal, retains his place, and leaders of the Jharkhand political movement are prominent.

The shame which the elite leaders feel for the traditional "pleasure" orientation is expressed in the following song:

After drinking rice beer,
After getting drunk,
A man walks with his *dhoti* falling to the ground.
Seeing all these bad things the aboriginal brother becomes sorrowful.

There are several reasons why the traditional "pleasure" orientation is opposed. As already suggested, it is an attribute of low status in the prevailing system of caste ranking, and the elite have internalized a distaste for it, especially for its more manifest appearances. For this reason they particularly oppose mixed dancing. As the songs above make plain, "pleasure" is felt to be a detriment to study, hard work, mobility, and the "progress" of tribals. Almost all Santal industrial workers condemn "too much pleasure," and even in remote villages it is generally felt that "pleasure" needs to be curtailed. However, it is only the educated, and not by any means all of them, who have deeply internalized this attitude and who can make it work for them. At a "fair" (*pata* in Hindi and Santali) more than half the Santal present said that fairs are bad; "at these fairs we only run around like dogs and spend our money"; but they were participating nevertheless and having considerable "pleasure."

It is a fact that many Santal fail in school because they are lured away from their studies by the traditional "pleasure" activities. Similarly, there are some absences without leave from TISCO and some instances of coming to work drunk which are the result of too much "pleasure," particularly during festivals. Through songs, plays, speeches, and even prayers, the new cultural movement has succeeded in making most Santal feel that they ought not to over-indulge; but it would be too much to say that it has succeeded in changing the dominant motif of Santal culture. However, the commitment to personal and tribal mobility and the inhibition of "pleasure" are continually reinforced by the obvious increase in the possibilities of advancement.

It is not yet common in the villages but everywhere apparent in the *bustees* and in Jamshedpur that fathers scold their children for wasting time and remind them that if they do not study they shall end up "throwing about dung" or performing other menial jobs requiring hard and undignified labor. Most

111

of the young children of Santal industrial workers aspire to a "sitting-down job," if not in Delhi then at least in TISCO. The tension induced by the conflict between rank improvement and the pleasure complex is evident in the demeanor of the young Santal trying to resist the old siren songs of their culture. The Santal of ordinary means recognizes that life is generally short and hazardous and that the path to success is arduous and the goal uncertain of attainment. Under such circumstances it is remarkable how many Santal are committed to rank improvement.

The disruptive force of "envy" and associated witchcraft has been attacked in two fashions. All but the most isolated Santal now believe that "envy," and with it witchcraft and much disease, will disappear as the Santal, especially their females, become educated. The rationale for this hope is that education will impart virtue and improve rank; how then will it be possible for the virtuous and prosperous to be envious? As the Santal point out, the "educated *diku* women do not practice witchcraft, so neither will ours once they are similarly educated."

The second anti-"envy" doctrine is more sophisticated, has Great-Traditional qualities, and is a genuine example of cultural innovation. It was developed by a brilliant Santal high-school graduate, Ragnath Murmu, who lived for some time in a *bustee*, where he carried on "cultural work"; he has since retired to his native village. According to his view, there are witches who practice witchcraft because of "envy." However, they can cause sickness only in a person who has committed some sin. The solution to the problem of illness which is caused in part by witchcraft and in part by one's own sin is to live a

112

virtuous life and to adhere scrupulously to the traditional religious practices.

Ragnath Murmu is one of the founders of a cultural organization known as *Sarna Dharam Semlet'*, i.e., Sacred Grove Religious Organization. This organization, which today is a spearhead of the cultural movement, is an offshoot of the Jharkhand party. It was established before the census of 1951 for the purpose of persuading the tribals of the region to return their religion as *"Sarna."* Just as Hindu organizations like Arya Samaj pressure for Hindu returns as a sign of national solidarity, so Semlet' was created to show the solidarity of tribals. The battle over cultural identification is waged by both sides but it is social identification which is chiefly at stake. Though Semlet' began its campaign only a short time before the 1951 census was taken, 237,310 tribals from the state of Bihar did return themselves as followers of the *"Sarna"* religion (Census of India, Vol. V. Bihar, Part II, A Tables, p. 309). There is, of course, no native word in any of the tribal languages which designates their religion, and the word *Sarna*, meaning Sacred Grove in Munda, has had to be officially chosen for the purpose. Since it is not even the word for Sacred Grove in Santali or Ho, it faces further difficulties, and if it is to be widely adopted it will require a good deal of explaining, especially to the mass of non-literate Santal and Hos.

Whatever its success in the census, under the leadership of Ragnath Murmu the organization has taken on a number of cultural functions, such as propagating Mr. Murmu's theory of witchcraft. While its chief ideologist is Mr. Murmu, its treasurer and secretary are TISCO workers. Among the officers only the secretary is illiterate, a deficiency for which he makes

113

up by being an ecstatic religious teacher known widely for his curing powers.

In the words of Esteemed Guru (*Guru Gomke*), a title conferred upon Ragnath Murmu by Jai Pal Singh, who is himself called Great Esteemed One (*Maran Gomke*), the purpose of Semlet' "is to teach the people to live peaceably with belief in the deities." The Guru has had some success in spreading the notion that Dhormo is the one all-embracing deity of which all others are a part, a theory like that of Vedantic monism. The socially centrifugal tendency of such a theory is, however, ingeniously mitigated by deriving the word Dhormo from the Santali terms, *doho* = to protect, *Hor* = a way, and *om* = to capture; hence "where there is a way of salvation" (salvation = *mafti*; Hindi). Thus the Guru makes *Dhormo*, a deity often worshipped along with the traditional ones, a Santal one after all. There is no end to the Guru's linguistic derivations of this variety, the scope of which is indicated by his derivation of Sanskrit from Proto-Mundari on the basis of structural similarities. Indeed, he argues that "many believe Valmiki Risi himself to have been a Santal."

The Guru has written a very long epic-heroic play, *Kherwar Bir*, which serves as a Santal equivalent of the Mahābhārata. The word *Kherwar* is an heroic designation for Santal; *Bir* means forest in Santali. The essence of the plot is that the Santal, then known as Kherwar and the possessors of a great kingdom, lose a war with a people who have the attributes of Hindus, the victors taking many members of the royal family prisoner. The Guru deftly reverses the usual Hindu pattern by having the Santals' opponents be cannibals prepared to eat their Santal prisoners. Fortunately, a young Kherwar prince, following the call of duty in spite of great danger, succeeds in both rescuing the prisoners and defeating the enemy. This play is both a parable about duty, and, like the old myth of the caste functions of the clans, a charter for present independence. In addition, the existence of such a written epic raises the rank value of Santal culture; to hear Santal praise the play is to erase all doubts about the significance of this objective. The historicity of the play is provided with archaeological support by sophisticated Santal who note that an abandoned old fort far to the north was probably the seat of the old kingdom. Less sophisticated Santal remark that the Guru did not make up the play, but that it was the result of revelation preceded by meditation, fasting, etc.

It is also the Guru who created the original Santal script. Numerous booklets explaining it have been distributed, and there are many Santal, particularly among the industrial workers, who can read it. Formerly all Santali writing was in Nagari, Bengali, or Roman script as developed by the missionaries. Wherever there are large gatherings today, Santal may be seen reading particularly the words to new songs in the new script. The connection of the script with solidarity is obvious to all; the Guru reports that he was asked by the former Mahārājā of Mayurbhanj to cease propagating the script because it was divisive; he claims to have replied that he would gladly do so if the Mahārājā would see to it that the Oriya script was also abandoned.

Several drama clubs have sprung up to perform *Kherwar Bir* and some other recent plays. One particularly interesting one is called *Olong*, or "Fate" (*Olong* = fate, Oriya) and concerns the schism between rich and poor. It urges magnanimity on the former and curtailment of "envy" and "pleasure" on the latter.

The great task that Semlet' hopes soon to undertake, and for which money is being collected, is to provide an authoritative text of Santal tradition written in the new script. At periodic Semlet' meetings one may observe eloquent representations of the cultural movement and its intimate connection with solidarity and the political rank path.

In place of traditional prayers such as: "Greetings, *Maran Buru*; in the name of this festival I offer you so do not allow any sickness, headache, or stomach ache to come. We give to you that we may remain in good health," one hears prayers more in keeping with an emergent "Great Tradition" such as the following: "Greetings, *Maran Buru*; be kind enough and pleased to accept my bowing and greeting. I prostrate myself before you and direct my attention to you. Come down as the wind and fly like a storm. Guide me in the path of righteousness. I bow down in all directions."

The following excerpts from typical speeches at Semlet' meetings give an "inside view" of the cultural movement and its social significance:

> In one village people stopped worshipping in the Sacred Grove and began to follow a Hindu sect which makes no offerings but only prays. Within three years they fell ill in every house. . . . Some "medicine man" from another village told them it is because you stopped worshipping in the Sacred Grove, so they returned to their old ways. Other people's religions will not make us strong. We should worship properly, then we can raise our religion so many will respect it.

> In ancient times it was said, and our "aboriginal" leaders also say, Sarna is our religion. The *diku* say our religion is Hindu. Then

116

what is our religion? If we celebrate with Hindus then we will soon be marrying them.

We will search out our traditions and publish our "precepts" [*bidhan* = precepts; Hindi]. . . . Many people are ashamed to "*Johar*" [a Santal greeting used for both persons and deities] at the Sacred Grove for fear the *dikus* will see. If we do not believe in our religion we will become Hindu or Christian. Now the *dikus* are trying to lure us away from our religion, so we must follow our Semlet' and all Santal will follow. We have to raise ourselves by religion and worshipping at the Sacred Grove. If we do not raise and support our religion we shall not progress in the "socio-political" [*somaj rajnita*; Hindi] sphere. This Semlet' is not different than the traditional religion. In the village of X, 300 people gathered for Semlet'; at that time an SDO [Sub-Divisional Officer] also came and that *diku* said, "this religion is not bad, it is a good thing."

Now we should rise like other people. The traditional religion is good but now we are following others' religion. We have no feeling for our caste and religion and that is why others are in high positions. If we have no unity and organization then others will have no respect for our caste. . . . Bihar police arrested twelve men for religious work. Now also they don't allow us to do religious work, but we must maintain our cow sacrifice at the Sacred Grove. Literacy and knowledge can help maintain our religion. When we spoke with the police who arrested the Santal they asked us for a written record of our religion. Then I said you can go village to village and ask people. Others drive hundreds and hundreds of cattle down the road and slaughter them and the police don't stop them. We sacrifice a cow every five years. This is our religion offering to Cando. . . . Other people try to destroy our religion but nobody should destroy any religion. I have seen in the constitution of India in the 25th chapter that no one shall be allowed to destroy a re-

117

ligion. . . . Some literate people also are leading us in a bad direction. In eating and clothing we often follow the *diku* way; we are departing from the way of our own society.

The final cultural manifestation to be discussed brings us back to the Durga Puja anecdote with which this chapter began. In the spirit of solidarity every effort is being made to prevent attendance at and participation in Hindu ceremonies. One of the dangers inherent in attendance and participation is the emulation of Hindu ways and the development of Hindu identification. The second danger stems from the manner of Santal participation, i.e., the Santal tendency to engage in mixed dancing, to become drunk, and in general to publicly display those forms of "pleasure" which are the attributes of low rank. The third danger bears a resemblance to the objection voiced by the city Santal, Mr. F., that the Santal are cheated by the clever *dikus*. No doubt there is some cheating, but what is really objectionable is that on such occasions considerable money is spent on "pleasure" and is thus not available for the serious business of rank improvement.

A more positive attempt to increase solidarity is the recent effort to get all Santal villages to celebrate their festivals simultaneously and to set the dates for such occasions so that they will not coincide with Hindu ceremonies. This effort has had a limited success in Mayurbhanj but has not been adopted generally because (1) the traditionally important visiting and reciprocity made possible by non-simultaneous ceremonies would have to be sacrificed, and (2) industrial workers now attending those of their own festivals which are held at the same time as Hindu ones on "free time" (permissible leave periods during which they are paid) would have to take leave without pay or forego all ceremonies. In principle, however, all agree that the recent proposal for simultaneity is one that ought to be implemented.

Mr. F., the acculturated city Santal raised by a Brahman family, was essentially opposed to attendance at the Durga Puja festival in Jamshedpur because of its danger to solidarity. His own acculturation and assimilationist tendencies were acquired before the opening of the political rank path. Today, despite some anxiety regarding the practice of certain distinctive practices, he is among the leaders of the movement for social solidarity and cultural separatism. No wonder that he should have complained, even though in error, about the passage in the Santal ethnography which seemed to him to say that "Santal only improve when in contact with Hindus."

The new solidarity fostered by political democracy is a new solidarity and not simply a return to traditional solidarity, at least for the immigrant industrial workers. It is they who are in the forefront of the movement, and there is no doubt that they are now bound to their people much more tightly than heretofore. But this does not make a *bustee* into a native village; it does not make marriage into a bond between kinship groups and villages; it does not eliminate the separate income and individual mobility of factory employment. In short, it does not recreate the traditional social basis for traditional solidarity. Instead it creates a new direct bond with all the Santal and to a somewhat lesser degree with all other tribals of the area. This new bond rests ultimately on the somewhat tenuous opportunity for the Santal and other tribals to function as a successful interest group. Given enough time, perhaps the new "likenesses" will be of enough force to hold the Santal and other tribals together in spite of change in the avenues of mobility.

4

the rank concession syndrome

Chapter 8 The Theory of the RCS

Solidarity which comes from likenesses is at its maximum when the collective conscience completely envelops our whole conscience and coincides in all points with it. But, at that moment, our individuality is nil. It can be born only if the community takes smaller toll of us. There are, here, two contrary forces, one centripetal, the other centrifugal, which cannot flourish at the same time. We cannot, at one and the same time, develop ourselves in two opposite senses. —If our ideal is to present a singular and personal appearance, we do not want to resemble everybody else.[1]

Santal historical experience suggests certain processes which may be applicable to all encysted societies which have conceded rank to a dominant surrounding society. It is these processes which I call the "rank concession syndrome" (RCS). "Rank concession" means the acceptance of social inferiority. "Acceptance" is an unfortunately ambiguous term, for it may occur in various degrees and perhaps even in a variety of forms.

---

[1] Durkheim 1933:130.

Nevertheless, to whatever degree and in whatever form such acceptance occurs, the syndrome becomes operative.

The evidence of Santal rank concession is manifold. It will be recalled that the earliest historical evidence shows the Santal adopting and abandoning traits on the basis of their rank value in Hindu society. The acceptance of alien rank values can hardly ensue without rank concession. The Santal themselves say that "the *diku* are big and knowing people" and their demeanor as they interact with Hindus, particularly of high caste, confirms acceptance in fair measure of their inferior status. Even today, in a period of renewed solidarity, the Santal are striving to "raise themselves" to the level of the "*diku*," as they say. The term *diku* is, of course, evidence enough of the ambivalence of the concession, and the history of Santal-Hindu relations has provided the Santal with sufficient reason to hate and fear as well as admire their Hindu neighbors. The earliest historical information indicates not only that rank concession must have begun considerably before British control, but that it was particularly pronounced among the traditional Santal elite. There is, for example, the myth of the Kisku king who became a Hindu and was forsaken by his fellows and the myth of Santal society constructed as a set of functionally specialized castes with each clan occupying a caste position.

To accept inferior status is to accept the attributes of rank of the superior society, and such acceptance produces a tendency to emulation. This emulation is an effect of rank concession, and evidence for it as well. The many examples noted of Santal emulation of the dominant Hindu society are to be understood as arising from the universal tendency of societies which have conceded rank to emulate. They may also be regarded as supporting evidence, to indicate rank concession, though rank

124

concession can be independently observed in Santal social relations with Hindus as well as inferred from Santal comments about the social superiority of the *diku*.

Such an emulative tendency, if put into practice, may at first lead to gross copying. Without internalization of emulative attitudes it is not likely to accomplish its objective and results in the kind of imitation epitomized by the *nouveau riche*. Such behavior appears gauche and thereby generates its own tendency toward internalization. Emulation may be directed toward attaining rank in interaction with social units belonging to the dominant society or within one's own society.

To concede that another society is more powerful is not tantamount to conceding it superior rank. Such a power concession generates its own borrowing tendencies, which might be termed "power incorporative borrowing," since it involves regarding the more powerful society's traits as possessing a special efficacy, which arises by projecting onto these traits the power of the dominant society. But while power concession does not imply rank concession, rank concession is almost always accompanied by and therefore implies power concession. Rank concession will therefore always be associated with both emulation and power incorporative borrowing. Emulation and power incorporation are often intermingled in particular acts and serve to maintain borrowed practices as well as to generate new borrowings. Power incorporation appears in its purest form in Santal curing practices, whose end is primarily curing efficacy or the belief in such efficacy, though the prestige which accrues to the practitioner who employs borrowed practices is not without significance. For example, one commonly hears Bengali and Oriya songs and Sanskritic prayers as essential elements in curing rites, though often even the practitioner does not understand the words. Such practices could hardly have been borrowed because of a peculiar "fit" of their content with traditional Santal patterns. Certainly such practices are not naturalistically more efficacious. It is rather a case of connecting status and efficacy which is expressed in the Santal reference to Hindus as "*big* and *knowing* people."

There is a third reason for the tendency to adopt practices of the dominant society, one which follows almost inevitably from the condition of being encysted. This is the "external pressure" brought to bear by the dominant society on the encysted society to adopt its customs. The basis for the near inevitability of this pressure is nothing less than the solidarity needs of the dominant society. Surrounding dominant societies must demand allegiance to at least the official symbols of suzerainty; acceptance of a number of other customs is likely also to be demanded as the solidarity needs of the dominant society increase. There are likely also to be a number of customs of the encysted society which the superior society finds repugnant, a reaction which invariably creates some pressure for "reform" of the encysted society. The pressures exerted on the encysted society may include positive rewards for compliance or coercive acts by police or even by an army.

Perhaps the oldest and most continuous of such pressures on the Santal has been governmental interference with Santal cow sacrifice and beef eating. Armed interference has been practiced everywhere and has not ceased under present democratic conditions. Cow sacrifice has continued, but in secret so as to avoid prosecution and interruption of the rites. However, some villages, fearing arrest and harassment, have abandoned such sacrifice, particularly where there are Hindus in the village who might report this activity to the authorities. There is no question that this pressure is the result of repugnance as well as solidarity needs.

The tendency to borrow which follows rank concession undermines solidarity, for all borrowing, by reducing distinctiveness, weakens solidarity, and borrowing of traits which directly represent solidarity is especially debilitating. Emulative borrowing not only eradicates boundary markers but is destructive of the internal aspect of solidarity, since it is likely to be more intense among segments of the encysted society with superior status. This differential emulation arises largely because of the following conditions: (1) the elite tend to have more intimate contact with members of higher social units because they are often representatives of their society in inter-societal relations, (2) they may attract a coterie belonging to higher social units but personally limited in political and economic power; such a coterie derives political and economic advantage from the relationship and confers prestige on its benefactor, (3) no amount of emulation in the absence of the requisite political and/or economic power can achieve rank improvement; the recognition of this fact contributes to differential emulation since the wealthy and powerful are the only ones in a position to attain higher rank in exogenous relations through emulation. Such differential emulation and the type of external relations described here have been noted among the Santal as well as other tribes in the area.

The impact of differential emulation on internal solidarity is to reduce "likeness" and to provide a cultural basis for divisive status distinctions. The ubiquitousness of "envy" and connected witchcraft in Santal social relations, and the difficulty of relations between the educated Santal elite and the non-elite exemplify this effect. The cultural gap between the traditional, uneducated elite and the ordinary Santal was not nearly so great, nor relations between them so strained.

In addition to the borrowing tendencies which flow from rank concession and the external pressure exerted on encysted societies, there is another centrifugal tendency inherent in being an encysted society: political-judicial encroachment. The increasing jurisdiction of Hindu courts and "village *panchayat*" over affairs formerly handled endogenously are an example; there are also such benefits as the issuance of scholarships, health protection and treatment, digging of tube wells, etc. These encroachments on areas formerly managed by the traditional social organization diminish its authority and importance and serve to attach the Santal more firmly to the surrounding society.

All of the borrowing tendencies which flow from rank concession plus external pressure and encroachment on encysted societies tend to diminish solidarity. If there were no countervailing forces, the world would long ago have become more culturally homogeneous and socially unified than it is. A highly potent force contributing to cultural distinctiveness derives from the necessity of preserving solidarity. Although the basis of solidarity has been widely explored by sociologists and structural anthropologists, there is one condition of solidarity-maintenance which has not received much attention, and it is decisive within the RCS. I refer to the relation between avenues of mobility, or rank paths, as I have called them, and the maintenance of solidarity: some rank paths support solidarity and some undermine or destroy solidarity. Emulation might be assigned to the class of destructive rank paths, but since it is never a successful path in the absence of political and/or economic power, it is not by itself likely to pose a serious threat to solidarity. What is crucial, then, to the maintenance of solidarity are the political and economic conditions of mobility.

In general, the pursuit of rank through political power by a society, whether by war or by winning elections, serves to support the society's solidarity. Increased political power promises rewards to everyone in the society, though it may be specially advantageous to an elite. To be achieved it requires cooperation and a solid front of opposition against competing societies; efforts will be made to counter centrifugal tendencies and to increase solidarity.

Pursuit of rank through economic improvement, at least within the context of an essentially market society, has the opposite effect. It is divisive because it encourages greater emulation on the part of those who have superior economic power. Furthermore, it not only does not require societal solidarity, but is commonly inhibited by internal ties which demand redistribution of economic gain and thereby prevent individual accumulation and investment. Unlike success in the political rank path, which promises rewards to all, economic success is essentially individual; its ultimate achievement is "passing," i.e., social absorption in the dominant society. If rank is pursued through individual economic gain, all of the centrifugal tendencies inherent in rank concession and being encysted not only are free to run their course but are even accelerated as the rank path itself contributes to the centrifugal pressure.

The choice among rank paths obviously depends in part upon the objective conditions of the alternatives. However, whatever choice is made, including the possibility of various combined efforts, the emulation-solidarity conflict cannot be wholly evaded. This, of course, is so because emulation is inherent in rank concession and because all societies manifest some pressure in behalf of solidarity. If a society is essentially pursuing an economic rank path, solidarity will decline and the conflict will either be reduced or remain constant, depending upon the intensity of the various centrifugal tendencies which are operative. But if such a society pursues a political rank path, the pressure for solidarity will increase, and since the pressure for emulation continues, the conflict is likely to become acute. There are, of course, the other centrifugal tendencies already mentioned which also conflict with solidarity, but emulation and solidarity are especially opposed within the political rank path because both are important means to rank improvement; it is a case of not being able to have one's cake and eat it too.

The conflict between emulation and solidarity which is engendered by rank concession has certain characteristic cultural consequences. These consequences may be understood as attempts to reduce the conflict by transforming emulated traits into somewhat distinctive ones or by claiming that they are actually indigenous. The latter practice is especially effective among tribal and peasant peoples where history-mythology is so commonly used to validate contemporary practice; all that is required is a demonstration that what is borrowed is in reality a forgotten indigenous custom. The transformation device used most often to "naturalize" borrowed practices is syncretism; occasionally there may be "innovative combination," in which the fusion of borrowed and native custom is accompanied by a change in both and something new emerges. All of these naturalizing practices allow a society to have some solidarity and emulation too. Since societies on an economic rank path tend to have increasingly diminished emulation-solidarity conflicts, they are likely to manifest increasingly less naturalization of borrowed customs. Instead of producing cultural movements, the culture of such societies is likely to become rapidly more like that of the dominant society. Societies on a political rank path, however, are likely to engage in considerable naturalization since the emulation-solidarity conflict will be more intense. If the conflict is intense enough, a cultural movement may ensue.

In order to check the centrifugal tendencies inherent in rank concession and being encysted, such movements seize on distinctive traits and give their practice a new emphasis; they may even invent new distinctive characteristics. Ideally, the traits emphasized will be attributes of low rank value in the dominant society since these will be most conspicuously distinctive; furthermore these traits serve best to bind the endogenous elite to those of ordinary rank and thereby to close the gap created by differential emulation. It is, of course, difficult for the elite to carry out such customs since it often requires them to re-adopt what they had long ceased to practice; in some instances they may even have to overcome hard-won antipathies. This difficulty is an aspect of the emulation-solidarity conflict which may also lead to innovation and generate energy for cultural creativity.

Consider the case of a society which after long pursuing rank on the economic rank path switches to a political path. The leaders of such a move are likely to be the elite since they are in a position to gain office should there be a political victory and are generally most adept at political maneuvering, in both their own and the wider, dominant society; but they also have the strongest tendency to emulate, and since they have long been engaged in the effort to secure economic gains, they will have managed to internalize thoroughly the values, beliefs, and even fundamental orientations of the dominant society. The leaders of such a movement are bound to have an intense emulation-solidarity conflict. Should a cultural movement develop under these conditions, it is bound to be marked not only by a re-emphasis of distinctive traits and the characteristic naturalizing tendencies which arise from the emulation-solidarity conflict, but also by strikingly innovative processes. For such an elite the only recourse which will simultaneously preserve distinctiveness and solidarity on the one hand, and express their own deep evaluations of what is true, beautiful, and worthy of rank on the other, is to produce their own "Great Tradition"; or they may borrow a distinctive one from some other society than the one in which they are encysted. If they create one of their own it is likely in fundamentals to be much like that of the dominant society but to differ conspicuously in lesser matters, retaining distinctive traditional practices. But even the fundamentals which are imported must be naturalized both to maintain distinctiveness and to penetrate successfully the non-elite. Such cultural creativity is likely to develop a momentum of its own as personal expression pride of creativity, and public recognition of culture-producers comes into play. Thus a cultural movement which begins largely as a means of strengthening solidarity so that political gains can be made may become genuinely creative, though it must continue to satisfy the requirements of its original impetus.

To return to Santal historical experiences, from the pre-British period in which rank concession began to the 1930's and the advent of political democracy, excluding brief periods of nineteenth-century rebellion, solidarity was increasingly undermined. Rank concession was producing emulation, differential emulation, and power-incorporative borrowing. The evidence suggests that migration was the chief means of responding to this pressure so as to maintain the integrity of Santal society. With British control, the spreading market, growing wealth differences, and external encroachment add to the previous centrifugal tendencies. Santal solidarity continued to be sufficient to permit the rebellions of the nineteenth century, but their crushing defeat, in the absence of democratic political opportunity, meant complete closure of the political rank path. Thereafter the decline of solidarity accelerated, and Hinduized sects began to develop. An additional centrifugal force, industrial development, appeared in the early part of this century among the southern Santal. It affected all of this population by accelerating economic opportunity and increasing education but had an additional disintegrative effect on migrant industrial workers.

Culturally, the entire period from pre-British times to political democracy is one of increasing Hinduization. Except for the brief periods of rebellion, from the time of British control to the 1930's the Santal pursued rank almost exclusively via economic mobility and emulation. The cultural consequence of this rank path plus the disintegrative tendencies inherent in rank concession and being encysted is to increase the "cultural load," i.e., to increase the number of borrowed traits which reduce distinctiveness and are internally the object of invidious comparison. This threat to internal solidarity was noted in the growing antipathy between rich and poor and the surpassing importance of "envy." On behalf of traditional solidarity, efforts were made to halt emulation and participation in Hindu ceremonies, but with limited success. There is also evidence from this period of the naturalizing processes which arise from the emulation-solidarity conflict. Nevertheless, the cultural load tended to increase, particularly in unaltered Hindu attributes of rank value.

The new political rank path of the 1930's, with its need for increased solidarity, created enough pressure through the emulation-solidarity conflict to generate a cultural movement. Not only were serious efforts made to curtail borrowing and to abandon emulative practices, but various emulative characteristics previously absorbed were naturalized. While distinctive traits of low rank value received new emphasis, the "Great Tradition" aspect of the movement imported essentially Hindu orientations into the culture, naturalizing them by means of innovative combination with traditional customs. The most striking examples of this have been the creations of "Esteemed Guru."

As an aid to thought the major principles of the RCS as applied to encysted societies are succinctly listed below. However, this condensed statement has required some obvious oversimplification and is not meant as a substitute for the more discursive discussion which precedes it.

The RCS as Applied to Encysted Societies*

1. The "cultural load" of the encysted society is inversely related to its solidarity and its ability to resist assimilation.
2. Rank concession produces a tendency to emulate; since emulation increases the cultural load, rank concession is also destructive of solidarity.
3. Emulation is likely to be of the differential variety.
4. A dominantly economic rank path decreases solidarity.

---

* All of the following propositions should be qualified by *ceteris paribus*.

5. A dominantly political rank path increases solidarity.

6. Differential emulation is more destructive of solidarity than random emulation; since the economic rank path is particularly conducive to differential emulation it is particularly destructive of solidarity.

7. Though power incorporative borrowing is at least analytically distinguishable from emulation, rank concession is always accompanied by power concession; therefore rank concession implies a tendency to power incorporative borrowing as well as emulation. (Power concession does not however imply rank concession.) Power incorporative borrowing also increases the cultural load.

8. Every society has some endogenous sources of solidarity; therefore every society that has conceded rank has an emulation solidarity conflict of some proportion.

9. Such a conflict manifests itself in a variety of characteristic ways, among which are the following:
   a) indigenous claims
   b) syncretism
   c) innovative combination
   d) pattern emulation—trait maintenance

10. An intense emulation-solidarity conflict may generate a "cultural movement."

11. A shift from a dominantly economic to a dominantly political rank path is likely to produce a severe emulation-solidarity conflict and may thereby serve to generate a cultural movement.

12. Encysted societies are subject to the following additional threats to their solidarity:
    a) political-judicial encroachment
    b) pressure to accept national solidarity symbols
    c) repugnance pressures

Chapter 9 Implications of the RCS

The force of emulation in spreading Indian culture has long been recognized in the voluminous literature on that country. Srinivas has conceptualized much of the thought on this subject in his discussion of "Sanskritization." He maintains that mobility has long been possible within the caste system, and that castes have risen by emulating high-caste behavior and high-caste restraints, such as vegetarianism and teetotalism. In his view this emulating process of Sanskritization has served to increase cultural uniformity within regional caste hierarchies and over the length and breadth of India.[1] Doubtless it has, yet without some force opposed to emulation, the very great cultural heterogeneity of contemporary India is difficult to comprehend.

The RCS suggests solidarity as the counterposed force. Solidarity is the force behind the maintenance and even the elaboration of distinctive traits; it also partially accounts for the characteristic transformation that many borrowed traits

---

[1] Srinivas 1952:202–227.

undergo, since according to the RCS this transformation is a result of the emulation-solidarity conflict.

In addition to posing a countervailing force, the RCS theory holds, in contradiction to Srinivas' position, that no amount of emulation will result in higher rank in the absence of the requisite political and/or economic power. It therefore shifts attention to the condition of political and economic rank paths as fundamental determinants of cultural development in hierarchically arranged societies.

Bose has elaborated a position which in some respects parallels the RCS. He suggests, with India and Britain in mind as well as Indian tribals, that culture tends to "flow from an economically dominant group to a poorer one when the two are tied together to form a larger productive organization through some historical accident."[2] While Bose stresses the primacy of economic power rather than rank, the direction of flow, i.e., from British to Indians or from Hindus to tribals, is the same as in Srinivas' formulation. Bose remarks that economic inferiority "has sapped at the root of national self-respect," which sounds much like the result of what I have termed rank concession.[3] The primacy which he gives to economic power might be incorporated in the RCS to close it just where I have left it open; this would be accomplished by arguing that it is economic power which ultimately produces rank concession. However, it is not certain that other forms of power, particularly political power, which are partially independent of economic power, might not accomplish the same end.

Marriott has most clearly recognized that processes running counter to emulation are necessary to account for the diversity

---

[2] Bose 1953:351.

[3] Bose, *ibid.*

which is so apparent in India. With compelling documentation he indicates not only the prevalence of great traditional Sanskritic practices at the village level but also simultaneously a tendency for little traditional, non-Sanskritic traits to retain their place. Following a suggestion of Redfield and Singer, he suggests that there is a flow upward from the little community to the great centers where the literati reside ("Universalization") as well as flow in the reverse direction ("Parochialization"). He emphasizes that transformation of what is received occurs at both levels. Adopting a cultural mode of analysis, he accounts for the maintenance of two traditions by the differing cultural screens of the two levels through which diffused traits must pass. The RCS theory suggests that solidarity pressures might also be responsible for the transformations which take place, and therefore for the maintenance of two distinct traditions. Many of the cultural variations within both little and great traditions which Marriott finds at the village level might similarly be accounted for.[4]

Much of anthropology, and through anthropology the other social science disciplines, have come to be dominated by the "configurational" theory of borrowing. This idea, made explicit and deservedly famous by Ruth Benedict in *Patterns of Culture*, suggests that what is borrowed by a culture either "fits" its configurations or is likely to be modified so as to fit. Though there is much evidence in favor of this theory, if it were the whole story, either there would be no change in cultural configurations or all such change would be essentially endogenous. Santal absorption of Hindu orientations and even of specific antipathies makes it clear that even configurations can be borrowed; a casual glance at the world today provides

---

[4] Marriott 1955.

innumerable additional examples, such as the Indians themselves and the Chinese Communists. Potentialities for rapid
cultural change are far greater than the configurational process
alone can take account of.

The RCS theory suggests that inherent in rank concession
are the potent forces of emulation and power-incorporative
borrowing, which contribute to the acceptance of "incongruent"
traits, i.e., traits that do not fit traditional configurations. This
is not to say that congruence is irrelevant, but that it may be
overridden in the pursuit of rank. The theory therefore helps
to explain why non-congruent traits are borrowed and under
what conditions. Besides making this kind of cultural flexibility intelligible, the RCS provides a partial explanation of
culture movements which are seen to be stimulated by the
emulation-solidarity conflict.

The RCS suggests new functions for what Herskovits has
referred to as reinterpretation and syncretism. Herskovits has
suggested that these transformations serve in "integrating borrowed elements into a recurring culture,"[5] a valuable insight
which nonetheless does not account for the borrowing of non-
congruent traits. Furthermore, as Herskovits himself says, such
"integration" frequently involves "new values" which change
the cultural significance of old forms.[6] It would seem that
cultural integration could better be maintained by rejection of
non-congruent borrowing, and it would appear that "new
values" could hardly be borrowed according to the configurational theory. The RCS adds considerations of social integration
and rank pursuit to those of cultural integration. The transformations which occur in borrowed material are therefore seen

---

[5] Herskovits 1949:553.

[6] Herskovits, *ibid.*

140

to arise from the social necessity of maintaining distinctiveness as well as the pressure of cultural integration. The borrowing of non-congruent practices and even "new values" is seen to arise from the pursuit of rank.

The RCS may also be used to supplement Park's formulation of the marginal man concept.[7] The RCS adds the dimension of social marginality to Park's cultural interpretation. Park's marginal man possesses cultural objectivity because he has experienced a culture other than his own; this experience releases him from the "cake of custom" and enables him to develop or participate in a new culture. "It is in the mind of the marginal man that the conflicting cultures meet and fuse" and where "the process of civilization may best be studied."[8] The RCS points out that identification with two societies is also at stake and that cultural choices are importantly related to this dimension of the decision. Social identification is in turn closely related to rank pursuit, and the creativity which characterizes the marginal man may, in part, result from the emulation-solidarity conflict.

Milton Singer and Fred Eggan have both called my attention to the fact there are important resemblances between the RCS and what sociologists generally refer to as the "reference group theory." Though it would be a task far beyond my present understanding to completely translate the RCS into the language of reference group theory, a few points of contact are perhaps worth mentioning. In his presentation on reference group theory, Robert K. Merton states that a question of central importance to a developing theory of reference group behavior is "under which conditions are associates within one's

---

[7] Park 1928.
[8] Park 1928:881.

own groups taken as a frame of reference for self-evaluation and attitude formation, and under which conditions do out-groups or non-membership groups provide the significant frame of reference."[9] The RCS offers some possible answers to this query by pointing to the various factors which tend to increase or decrease the solidarity of a group; in particular the theory of the RCS would suggest that avenues of mobility are among the crucial determinants in choosing a reference group. Merton also raises as a central issue the question of how "divergent or even contradictory norms and standards" of different reference groups are resolved.[10] Here the RCS provides a partial answer in terms of the resolving characteristics accompanying the emulation-solidarity conflict. Obviously the language of reference group theory and its applications are far broader than that of the RCS, so that all the advantages are on the side of translating the RCS into reference group conceptual framework. Unfortunately that is a formidable task which for the present will have to remain undone.

Industrial Employment and the RCS

Not only have anthropologists overemphasized the configurational theory within the discipline but they have succeeded widely in convincing their other social science colleagues that culture is indeed nearly unshakable. At many conferences on economic development in underdeveloped areas there is an anthropologist who presents the configurational theory with a few well chosen anecdotes to make the point. A favorite supporting tale is about the Africans who filled their wheelbarrows

[9] Merton 233.
[10] Merton, *ibid.*

with earth and then put them on their heads! In partial defense of such anthropologists it is well to recognize that their tales are often meant to deter overzealous non-anthropologists from insensitively smashing what to anthropologists are attractive native cultures.

The successful transference of anthropological beliefs and even configurations to other disciplines is well illustrated in Wilbert Moore's authoritative work, *Industrialization and Labor*, which deals with tribal and peasant peoples as a working force. Speaking of their ability to adapt to industrial conditions, he has this to say:

> Transference is facilitated by an overall similarity of the culture in contact, or as a corollary, by a similarity of the specific new elements and the pre-existing elements serving approximately the same goals or functions. As a practical matter of inducing cultural change, spontaneous acceptance is a function of similarity. The more unsuitable the existing circumstances the more necessary it will be to rely on slow fermentation than on rapid effervescence.[11]

While not disputing the relevance of congruence, the RCS suggests dynamics of borrowing which make it possible to understand how even pervasive configurations of a culture (such as the pleasure complex among the Santal) may be fundamentally modified. The notion of highly stable configurations which persist in spite of numerous changes in specific traits seems less applicable to societies which have conceded rank than to societies which have not. Given appropriate social circumstances, such as the separation from their own people which the Santal tend to encounter in Hindu-dominated

---

[11] Moore 1951:189–190.

schools, one may anticipate the borrowing of basic orientations or configurations as well as specific traits. The RCS then, suggests one way in which cultures may change without remaining really the same; the anticipation of the possibility of such radical change in societies which have conceded rank is of obvious importance in understanding adaptability to economic development.

In the absence of an open political rank path, industrial employment has been shown to diminish solidarity. This decline is chiefly due to the following conditions: (1) increased education which furthers the emulation gap; (2) separate income plus migration, a combination which severs traditional ties; (3) the time demands of industrial employment; (4) dispersal of the community and inappropriate facilities in the urban environment.

In the presence of an open political rank path, industrial employment may contribute substantially to a new solidarity. This effect is chiefly the result of increased education, which makes members of the industrial community the most appropriate representatives of their community and hence those who have the most direct interest in political victory and solidarity. Since they are also likely to be among the most acculturated, it is in the industrial centers where the emulation-solidarity conflict is most intense and therefore where the center of cultural development is likely to be.

The RCS provides a tool for analyzing the prospect of recruitment and commitment of an industrial labor force from an encysted society which has conceded rank. As I have indicated elsewhere,[12] the Santal have readily made themselves available for employment at Jamshedpur since the founding

---

[12] Orans 1959.

of the city. Furthermore, there being no economic advantage in their making seasonal shifts from farm to industrial labor, they have been reasonably steady workers. Yet everywhere in the literature on tribals and peasants in industry there is discussion of heavy turnover and absenteeism. One of the chief causes of this unsteadiness is said to be the preference for leisure rather than increased income resulting in the traditional backward-bending supply curve for labor. Traditional Santal culture has been shown to have an unusually heavy commitment to "pleasure"; why then do the Santal not fit the stereotype of the tribal industrial worker?

To be sure, a large number of Santal must work steadily at Jamshedpur or be discharged and starve. However, figures cited here and elsewhere show that many might have remained in their native villages without unusual hardship. Perhaps it may be concluded that a sufficient condition for developing an adequate and steady labor force from tribal peoples is that it be drawn from societies which have conceded rank, assuming, of course, that pay and working conditions are adequate. Such societies will have developed strong emulative tendencies, and the consequent gap between the available economic means and the exogenous goals to be emulated (which are much more likely to require purchase, and thereby involvement in the money economy, than endogenous ones) may be wide enough to ensure considerable industrial commitment.

The switch from an exclusively economic rank path to a combined economic and political one may well result in a social and cultural movement as described. Such movements, which will be led by the elite, are likely to produce a rapid diffusion within the encysted society of emulated traits. The cultural resurgence which ensues may well result in such "revitaliza-

145

tion" as to have a positive effect on labor morale; this was certainly evident among the Santal. In general, any increase in the probability of mobility will serve to curtail pleasure and encourage rank pursuit; no doubt the reverse is also true.

The RCS in Newly Emergent Nations

The RCS has special relevance to the conditions generally prevailing in newly emergent nations. By virtue of being new, if nothing else, these nations are particularly hard-pressed to establish national solidarity. At the same time these nations typically begin their independence containing a number of encysted societies, each having in various degrees maintained a separate identity. Under such tension culture is especially likely to become a tool of opposing societal interests. If there is substantial political democracy it may be anticipated that encysted societies will show strong signs of preserving their identities and maintaining and accentuating distinctive traits. If rank concession exists, such "nativism" on the part of encysted societies ought to show signs of the naturalization processes characteristic of the emulation-solidarity conflict. The dominant national society may also be expected to "use" culture, fostering and even developing, if necessary, customs to symbolize and bind together the new national solidarity. In the absence of political democracy it would seem that opportunities of economic advance in the context of a market society would favor assimilation and national solidarity; this observation, however, is by no means meant as a recommendation.

References

Bodding, Paul Olaf. *Traditions and Institutions of the Santals,* being a translation of Horkoren mare Hapramko reak' Katha. (Oslo Universitet Ethnografiske Museum Bulletin 6.) Oslo: Oslo Universitet Ethnografiske Museum, 1942.

Bose, Nirmal Kumar, "The Hindu Method of Tribal Absorption," *Cultural Anthropology and Other Essays.* Calcutta: Indian Associated Publishing Co. Ltd., 1953.

Census of India, 1931, Behar and Orissa, VII, Part II, Table XVIII, 157–159.

Culshaw, W. J. *Tribal Heritage.* London: Lutterworth Press, 1949.

Culshaw, W. J. and Archer, W. G. "The Santal Rebellion," *Man in India,* Vol. XXV, 1945.

Dalton, E. T. *Descriptive Ethnology of Bengal.* Calcutta: 1872.

Datta, Kalikinkar. *The Santal Insurrection of 1855–57.* Calcutta: University of Calcutta, 1940.

Datta-Majumder, Nabendu. *The Santal: A Study in Culture-Change.* Department of Anthropology, Government of India, Memoir No. 2. Published by the Manager of Publications, Delhi, 1955.

Durkheim, Emile. *On the Division of Labor in Society.* Translated by George Simpson. New York: The Macmillan Company, 1933.

147

Herskovits, Melville J. *Man and His Works.* New York: Alfred A. Knopf, 1949.

Merton, Robert K. *Social Theory and Social Structure,* revised edition. Glenview, Ill.: The Free Press, 1957.

Mukherjea, C. L. *The Santals.* Publisher and year unknown.

Marriott, McKim. "The Little Communities in an Indigenous Civilization," *Village India.* Publisher and year unknown.

Moore, Wilbert E. *Industrialization and Labor.* Ithaca and New York: Cornell University Press, 1951.

Nash, Manning. *Machine Age Maya,* Memoir No. 87, The American Anthropologist, April, 1958.

Orans, Martin. "A Tribal People in an Industrial Setting," *Traditional India: Structure and Change.* Publication of the American Folklore Society, Bibliographical Series, Vol. X. Philadelphia, 1959.

Park, Robert E. "Human Migration and the Marginal Man," *American Journal of Sociology,* XXXIII, 881–893, May, 1928.

Polanyi, Karl. *The Great Transformation.* Beacon Hill, Boston: Beacon Press, 1957.

Redfield, Robert and Singer, Milton. "The Cultural Role of Cities," *Economic Development and Cultural Change,* Vol. III, No. 1:53073, 1954.

Roy, S. C. *The Mundas and Their Country.* Calcutta: City Book Society, 1912.

Srinivas, M. N. *Religion and Society Among the Coorgs of South India.* Oxford: Clarendon Press. (n.d.)

Sinha, Surajit. "Tribal Cultures of Peninsular India as a Dimension of the Little Tradition: A Preliminary Statement," *Traditional India: Structure and Change.* Publication of the American Folklore Society, Bibliographical Series, Vol. X. Philadelphia, 1959.

Thornton, Edward. *The History of the British Empire in India*, Vol. V. London: Wm. H. Allen and Co., 1843.

Weber, Max. *The Protestant Ethic and the Spirit of Capitalism.* London: George Allen and Unwin, 1930.

Index

Aboriginal, political party. *See* Jharkhand, political party
Aboriginal, state. *See* Jharkhand, state
Acculturation and assimilation, x. *See also* Hinduization
Acculturation, attitude towards, 96. *See also* Hinduization
Ādibāsī. See Aboriginal; *Ādibāsī* Cooperative Society, 102
Agriculturists, xi
Ancestor worship, 73, 80, 84
Archer, 32n. *See also* Culshaw and Archer
Arya Samaj, 90, 113

Baha (festival), 74–82
Benedict, R., 139
Bhitar, 24, 84
Bhumij, 28, 29, 30, 90
Bihar, 99, 100
Bodding, 4n, 36n
Boṅga (deities), 38, 75
Bose, 138n
"Boundary deities" (*sima boṅga*), 20, 77
Bride price, 61–62
Bustee, xii, *et passim*

Cando (deity), 7, 17
Caste, xi, xii, 28–29, 35, 42

Ceremonies, decline in *bustee* and city, 73–86. *See also* Festivals
Chotanagpur Plateau, x, 39, 88, 97, 100
"Clan" (*Paris* or *Jāti*), 10n, 13, 14, 20; sub-clan, 11n, 13, 20
Class, xii
Company houses, xiii, 74, 84
Configurational theory, 139–143
Consensus, 18–19
Corporate groups, xii, 13, 16
Court, 21
Cow sacrifice and beef eating, 27, 52, 107, 117, 126
Culshaw, 4n, 7n, 89n, 90
Culshaw and Archer, 31, 32n, 33n
Cultural creativity, x, 93, 101, 104; and political rank path, 106–107. *See also* Jharkhand political party, and Culture creativity

Dalton, 4n, 37n
Damodar River, 14, 15, 16
Dancing, 7, 9, 27, 29, 107
Datta, 31n
DB. *See Diku bapla*
Deko (*Diku*), 33n, *et passim*
Deredih, xiv, *et passim. See also Bustee*
Dhorom, 89, 106

151

Dhoti cloth, 61, 62, 110
Diba and Kisun, 34
Diku bapla (duar bapla, arranged marriage), 59–68
Durga Pyja (festival), 38, 93–97 *passim*; and solidarity, 118–119
Durkheim, 3n, 123n

Eating of beef, 51, 52. *See also* Cow sacrifice and beef eating
Economic rank path, 129–135
Eggan, F., 141
Education, 47 ff; motivation, 48; number of aborigine pupils, 50; solidarity, 51 ff. *See also* Solidarity, and Hinduization
Emergent nations, 146
Emulation, 124–135; differential, 42–43, 127–128
"Emulation-solidarity conflict," 56, 103–104, 127–146. *See also* "Rank-concession syndrome"
English, relations with, 30–32, 39
Envy (*hisạ*), 40, 53, 55, 112, 123, 133

F., Mr., 93–96, 118–119
Family, extended, 11, 22–24; nuclear, 11, 23
Fanderkuta, xiv, *et passim*
Female, attitude towards, 22–24, 112
Festivals, 9, 24; Hindu, 38–39, 88–89, 93–97 *passim*; male, 22; regional, 22. *See also* Ceremonies, and individual headings
"Field worship" (*thandi boṅga*), 13–14, 16
"Five People." *See* Village representatives
Funerary rites, 14–16

Gonok' hoṛ. See Relatives, joking
Gonoṅ. See Brideprice

Goram Boṅga (deity), 75, 76
"Great tradition," ix, xiv, 104, 105, 108–116 *passim*, 132
Guru, 114–115, 134

Hạndi, See Rice beer
Herskovits, 140n
Hindus, relations with, 27ff; ambivalence towards, 33. *See also* Hinduization
Hinduization, 29ff; differential, 41–43, 50–56. *See also* Emulation, Emulation-solidarity conflict, and Sanskritization
Hisa. See Envy
Ho, 5, 30
Household, 23, 24

Ignorant-illiterate, 50, 52, 54, 95
Industrial development, 47
Industrial employment, 144, 145
Industrialization and labor, 143
Industry, xii. *See also* Tata Company
"inner room" (*bhitạr*), 22, 8
Ituṭ' bapla (capture marriage), 42

Jaher. See Sacred Grove
Jaherera, 7, 75
Jamshedpur, xii, *et passim*
Jāti. See Clan
Jharkhand, aboriginal state, 97, 98–99, 100
Jharkhand, political party, 96–109
Jogmañjhi. See Village assistant headman
Johar, 76, 117
"Justice," 21

Karam (festival), 38
Kharswan, xii, xiv, 88, 97
"Kinsmen" (*peṛa hoṛ*), 16
Kinship, "fictitious," 10, 11, 12
Kinship organization, 9–25. *See also* individual headings

Language, 6, 28, 29
"Likeness," 3, 10, 24, 41, 97, 119, 127. *See also* Solidarity
Lineage, local, 11–20
Liṭa (deity), 7, 75, 76
Literacy, 41, 47; rate, 48
"Little tradition," ix
Location, Santal, xi

McPherson, 33n
Majumder, 37n
Man (author), 31
Mąñjhi. *See* Village headman
Mąñjhithan, 19, 77
Mąñjhi-Harąm. See Oldman Headman
"Maraṅ Buru" (deity), 6–7, 14, 24, 75, 76, 110, 116
"Marginal man," 141
Market, x, xiv, 15–16, 39–43, 87, 133. *See* Solidarity
Marriage, 13, 21, 58–73; marriage form and *bustee* residence, 68; and per capita income, 66; and village residence, 65. *See also Diku bapla, Itut' bapla, Nápam bapla, Sange bariat,* and *Tunki dipil*
Marriott, 43n, 138, 139
Mayurbhanj district, xii, xiv, 34, 47, 49, 89, 97, 98, 100
Member of Bihar Legislative Association, 100, 106, 107
Merton, R. K., 141, 142n
Migration, 57–58, 81, 85–86
Migration to industrial employment, xiv, 58, 71 ff. *See also* Solidarity
MLA. *See* Member of Bihar Legislative Association
"Modernization," 73
Moore, W., 143n
Mōre hor. See Village representatives
Mōreko (deity), 7, 75
Mukhurjea, 50

Munda, 5, 30, 34, 97
Mundari-speaking people, 6, 7, 9, 28, 97
Murmu, Ragnath, 112–114
Myth of creation, 4, 5, 9
Mythological history, 35–36

Naeke. See Village priest
Nápam bapla (unarranged marriage), 63–73
Nash, M., 57n, 85
Naturalization process, 130, 133, 134
NB. *See Napam bapla*

"Oldman Headman" (*Mąñjhi-Harąm*), 19, 77, 81
Orans, 53n, 144n
Orissa, x, 88, 99

Pargana, 6, 10, 20, 21, 32
Parganaths (multi-village headmen), 10, 20, 21, 42
Paris. See Clan
Parke, 141n
"Parochialization," 43, 139
Patrilineal kinship, x, xi, 23
Patterns of Culture, 139
Per-capita income, 70
Pera hor. See Kinsmen
"Pleasure complex" (*rąska*), 7–9, 20, 21, 27, 41, 43, 108, 110, 111, 115; differential, 52–53
Polanyi, 31n
Political democracy, x, xiv, 98, 132, 133, 146
Political rank path, 90, 93 ff. *See also* Jharkhand political party
Population, Santal, xi
"possessed" (*rum*), 14, 75
"Power incorporative borrowing," 125, 133
Pradhān. See Village headman

153

Ranchi District, 34, 97
"Rank-concession syndrome," x, 123–145
RCS. *See* "Rank-concession syndrome"
Rebellions, Santal, 30–37, 47, 133
Redfield and Singer, ix, 104n, 139
Reference group theory, 141, 142
Regional cultural and social interaction, 22
"Relatives, joking" (*gonok' hoṛ*), 75, 78
Religious identification, 87–90; per cent Hindu, 88
Resources, xi
Rice beer (*hạndi*), 5, 8, 22, 24, 85
Rice crop, xi
Roy, 30n, 88n
Rum. See "Possessed"

"Sacred Grove" (*Jaher*), 6, 19, 73–84 *passim*, 106n, 116, 117; national shared deities of, 7n. *See also Sarna Dharam Semleṭ'*
Sakrat (festival), 39, 82
"Sanskritization," 137
Saṅge bạriạt (arranged marriage), 62–68, 71
Sarna Dharam Semleṭ' (Sacred Grove Religious Organization), 113–117
Sarna Dhorom, 106n
SB. *See Saṅge bạriạt*
Secularization, 59, 74, 78, 80
Sendra (territorial gathering), 22
Seraikela, xii, xiv, 88, 97
Sido and Kanhu, 32, 33, 34
Singer, M., 73n, 104n, 139, 141
Singh, Jai Pal, 97, 98, 109, 114
Singhbhum district, xii, xiii, 47, 88
Sinha, 7, 28, 29n
Socio-cultural resurgence. *See* Cultural creativity

Sohrae (festival), 81–82
Solidarity, 3 ff; external, 4, 27 ff; decrease of, 47, 90; Durkheim's discussion of, 3, 123; internal, 3 ff; new, 119
Srinivas, 137n, 138

Tata Iron and Steel Company (TISCO), xii, 47, 83, 85, 93, 102
Tata Workers Union, xii, 102
TD. *See Ṭunki dipil*
Territorial organization, xi, 10. *See also* Pargana
Thandi boṅga. See Field worship
Thornton, 34n
Tola, 10, 78
Tribe, 10, 12, 24
Ṭunki dipil (arranged marriage), 63–68 *passim*
Tureko (deity), 7

"Universalization," 43, 139
Urban industrial effects, xiv, 43. *See also* Migration to industrial employment

Village, xi, 10, 17–21 *passim*
Village assistant headman (*jogmạñjhi*), 10, 61, 78
Village headman (*Mạñjhi*), 10, 17–19 *passim*, 61
Village priest (*Naeke*), 10, 17–19 *passim*, 75–77 *passim*
Village representatives (*mõre hoṛ*), 18, 60, 76n

Wealth differences, 24–25, 39 ff. *See* Solidarity
Weber, M., 57n, 85
Witchcraft, 54, 55, 112

The manuscript was edited by Faith Schmidt and Richard Dey. The book was designed by Peter Nothstein. The type face for the text is Garamond designed by Claude Garamond around 1532. The display face is Rondo Bold designed by Stefan Schlesinger and Dick Dooijes in 1948.

The book is printed on Glatfelter's RRR antique paper and bound in Joanna Mills Veltex vellum cloth over boards. Manufactured in the United States of America.